Survey of Library Services for Distance Learning Programs

ISBN: 1-57440-098-3

Table of Contents

List of Participants

Arizona Western College
Benedictine University
Bergen Community College
Boston Architectural College
California State University, Dominguez Hills
Carroll Community College
Centennial College (Canada)
Central Michigan University
Century College
Citrus College
Coastline Community College
Columbia Gorge Community College
Confederation College (Canada)
Dowling College
Drexel University
East Carolina University
Empire State College
Fairleigh Dickinson University Library
Fielding Graduate University
Glendale Community College Library Media Center
Gonzaga University
Guilford Technical Community College
Gulf Coast Community College
Informatio (Ukraine)
Jackson State Community College
James Cook University
Lake Erie College of Osteopathic Medicine
Lassen Community College Library
Liberty University
McKillop Library, Salve Regina University
Medicine Hat College (Canada)
Mineral Area College
Morris Library, Southern Illinois University Carbondale
Mount Saint Vincent University (Canada)
Mount Wachusett Community College Library
Mt. San Antonio College

Nashotah House
New Jersey Institute of Technology
North Dakota State College of Science
North Seattle Community College
Northern Maine Community College
Nova Scotia Community College (Canada)
Oregon Health and Science University
Pace University Library
Panola College
Pellissippi State Technical Community College
Pikes Peak Community College
Randolph Community College Library
Saddleback College Library
San Juan College
Santa Barbara Business College
Seattle Pacific University
Sheffield Hallam University (UK)
Sheridan College
Simon Fraser University Library (Canada)
South Dakota School of Mines & Technology
Southeastern Oklahoma State University
Springfield College
St. Cloud State University
St. John's University Library
Suffolk County Community College
Sullivan University
Texas A&M University-Commerce Library
Texas A&M University-Corpus Christi
The Art Institute of Pittsburgh
The College of Nursing (Australia)
Thompson Rivers University (Canada)
Thrift LIbrary of Anderson University
Tri-County Community College
Trinity Western University (Canada)
Tyndale University College & Seminary (Canada)
University of Arkansas at Little Rock
University of Calgary (Canada)

University of Central Lancashire (U.K.)
University of Georgia Libraries
University of Idaho Library
University of Illinois at Springfield
University of Nebraska Medical Center
University of New Brunswick Libraries
    (Canada)
University of North Carolina, Charlotte
University of Regina (Canada)
University of Richmond
University of South Florida St.
    Petersburg
University of South Florida Tampa
    Library

University of Southern California
University of St. Andrews (U.K.)
University of Tennessee, Knoxville
University of Wisconsin-Eau Claire
University of Wisconsin-Whitewater
University of Wyoming Libraries
Utah State University
Viterbo University
Walden University
Washington State University
Wayne Community College
Wesley College

List of Tables

Sample Dimensions

U.S. and Non-U.S. Libraries

	U.S.	Non-U.S.
Entire Sample	80.81%	19.19%

Carnegie Class

	Community College	4-Year Degree Granting College	MA or PhD Granting College	Research University
Entire Sample	34.34%	8.08%	35.35%	22.22%

Public or Private Status

	Public College	Private College
Entire Sample	73.74%	26.26%

Number of FTE Students at the Institution

	>12,000	6,001-12,000	2,500-6,000	<2,500
Entire Sample	25.25%	25.25%	25.25%	24.24%

Number of FTE Distance Learners

	>2,000	1,000-2,000	250-999	<250
Entire Sample	23.08%	24.36%	25.64%	26.92%

Percentage of Distance Learners Living More than 50 Miles from Campus

	80-100%	51-79%	25-50%	1-24%
Entire Sample	27.71%	20.48%	27.71%	24.10%

Chapter One: Virtual Reference

Virtually all libraries surveyed offered an email response box as a virtual reference service, with large public colleges leading the way. Just under 85% of private colleges and 97% of private colleges offered an email address for virtual reference queries. Institutions generally were more likely to offer this service the larger their FTE student population. This was even more true for schools with larger FTE distance learning students. All colleges with more than 12,000 FTE students or 2,000 FTE distance learners had such a service.

Just over half of the libraries offered real-time chat as a virtual reference service. Fewer private colleges, 46%, offered the service, compared to almost 55% of the public colleges. There was a larger difference between U.S. libraries and non-U.S. libraries, 49% and 68% of which, respectively, offered a virtual reference chat service.

Availability of real-time chat at colleges generally increased as FTE student populations increased. The drop in availability was precipitous as the number of FTE distance learners decreased, however. Of the colleges with fewer than 250 FTE distance learners, just 38% offered real-time chat as a virtual reference service. Just 45% of colleges with between 250 and 999 distance learners reported the same, as did 68% of colleges with 1,000 to 2,000 distance learners and 61% of colleges with over 2000.

Almost 62% of respondents do not keep track of their distance learners' use of virtual reference services or compare them with the habits of traditional students. Of those respondents who did keep track, the most typical answer was that distance learners and traditional students used the virtual reference services to the same extent. Half as many reported that distance learners used the services less than traditional students, while just under 6% reported that distance learners use their services more than traditional students.

U.S. and non-U.S. libraries did not report significantly different findings. Compared to between 60 and 69% of the other institution types, just a third of the four-year degree granting colleges kept track of these statistics. Half of all the four-year degree granting colleges reported that use of virtual refernce by distance learners and traditional students was the same, but just 29% of community colleges, under 14% of MA or PhD-granting colleges and just under 15% of research universities reported this.

Research universities and MA or PhD-granting colleges were the only institution type to report that their distance learners used the virtual reference services more than traditional students used them. A higher percentage of private colleges, 15%, reported that distance learners used these services less than traditional students, compared to under 10% of public colleges.

The higher the enrollment, the more likely it was for an institution to keep track of their distance learners' usage habits of the virtual reference services offered by the library. Just over 52% of institutions with over 12,000 FTE students reported that they did not keep track of these statistics, compared to 60% of institutions with 6,001 to 12,000 FTE students, 61.9% of institutions with 2,500 to 6,000 FTE students, and 72.73% of institutions with fewer than 2,500 FTE students. Similarly, institutions with larger FTE student enrollments also tended to report that their distance learners and traditional students used their virtual reference services to the same extent. None of those institutions with fewer than 2,500 FTE students reported that distance learners use their virtual reference services more than traditional students do, but 5% of those with between 2,500 and 6,000 FTE students and 10% of institutions with over 6,000 FTE students reported the same.

Institutions with the highest FTE distance learners, over 2,000, were also most likely to both keep track of their distance learners' virtual reference service usage habits and to report that they were the same as those habits of traditional students'.

The percentage of the college's distance learners that lived more than 50 miles away from campus directly corresponded to how much the college kept track of their distance learners' virtual reference service usage. Just 44% of programs where the 80 to 100% of the distance learners lived more than 50 miles away did not keep track of these services, compared to 53% of colleges where 51-79% of their distance learners lived more than 50 miles away, 70% of colleges where 25-50% of their distance learners lived more than 50 miles away, and 67% of colleges where 1-24% of their distance learners lived more than 50 miles away.

Table 1.1:   Percentage of Libraries that Offer an Email Response Box as a Virtual Reference Service

	Yes	No
Entire Sample	93.94%	6.06%

Table 1.2:   Percentage of Libraries that Offer an Email Response Box as a Virtual Reference Service, Broken Out by U.S. and Non-U.S. Libraries

U.S. and Non-U.S. Libraries	Yes	No
U.S.	93.75%	6.25%
Non-U.S.	94.74%	5.26%

Table 1.3:   Percentage of Libraries that Offer an Email Response Box as a Virtual Reference Service, Broken Out by Carnegie Class

Carnegie Class	Yes	No
Community College	94.12%	5.88%
4-Year Degree Granting College	87.50%	12.50%
MA or PhD Granting College	91.43%	8.57%
Research University	100.00%	0.00%

Table 1.4:   Percentage of Libraries that Offer an Email Response Box as a Virtual Reference Service, Broken Out by Public or Private Status

Public or Private Status	Yes	No
Public College	97.26%	2.74%
Private College	84.62%	15.38%

Survey of Library Services for Distance Learning Programs

Table 1.5: Percentage of Libraries that Offer an Email Response Box as a Virtual Reference Service, Broken Out by Number of FTE Students at the Institution

Number of FTE Students at the Institution	Yes	No
>12,000	100.00%	0.00%
6,001-12,000	92.00%	8.00%
2,500-6,000	96.00%	4.00%
<2,500	87.50%	12.50%

Table 1.6: Percentage of Libraries that Offer an Email Response Box as a Virtual Reference Service, Broken Out by Number of FTE Distance Learners

Number of FTE Distance Learners	Yes	No
>2,000	100.00%	0.00%
1,000-2,000	94.74%	5.26%
250-999	95.00%	5.00%
<250	80.95%	19.05%

Table 1.7: Percentage of Libraries that Offer an Email Response Box as a Virtual Reference Service, Broken Out by Percentage of Distance Learners Living More than 50 Miles from Campus

Percentage of Distance Learners Living More than 50 Miles from Campus	Yes	No
80-100%	91.30%	8.70%
51-79%	100.00%	0.00%
25-50%	91.30%	8.70%
1-24%	95.00%	5.00%

Table 1.8: Percentage of Libraries that Offer a Real Time Chat Service as a Virtual Reference Service

	Yes	No
Entire Sample	52.53%	47.47%

Table 1.9: Percentage of Libraries that Offer a Real Time Chat Service as a Virtual Reference Service, Broken Out by U.S. and Non-U.S. Libraries

U.S. and Non-U.S. Libraries	Yes	No
U.S.	48.75%	51.25%
Non-U.S.	68.42%	31.58%

Table 1.10:   Percentage of Libraries that Offer a Real Time Chat Service as a Virtual Reference Service, Broken Out by Carnegie Class

Carnegie Class	Yes	No
Community College	47.06%	52.94%
4-Year Degree Granting College	37.50%	62.50%
MA or PhD Granting College	48.57%	51.43%
Research University	72.73%	27.27%

Table 1.11:   Percentage of Libraries that Offer a Real Time Chat Service as a Virtual Reference Service, Broken Out by Public or Private Status

Public or Private Status	Yes	No
Public College	54.79%	45.21%
Private College	46.15%	53.85%

Table 1.12:   Percentage of Libraries that Offer a Real Time Chat Service as a Virtual Reference Service, Broken Out by Number of FTE Students at the Institution

Number of FTE Students at the Institution	Yes	No
>12,000	60.00%	40.00%
6,001-12,000	52.00%	48.00%
2,500-6,000	48.00%	52.00%
<2,500	50.00%	50.00%

Table 1.13:   Percentage of Libraries that Offer a Real Time Chat Service as a Virtual Reference Service, Broken Out by Number of FTE Distance Learners

Number of FTE Distance Learners	Yes	No
>2,000	61.11%	38.89%
1,000-2,000	68.42%	31.58%
250-999	45.00%	55.00%
<250	38.10%	61.90%

Table 1.14:   Percentage of Libraries that Offer a Real Time Chat Service as a Virtual Reference Service, Broken Out by Percentage of Distance Learners Living More than 50 Miles from Campus

Percentage of Distance Learners Living More than 50 Miles from Campus	Yes	No
80-100%	43.48%	56.52%
51-79%	70.59%	29.41%
25-50%	47.83%	52.17%
1-24%	60.00%	40.00%

Table 1.15:   Use of Virtual Reference Services by Distance Learners vs. Traditional Students

	Use the service less than traditional students	Use it about the same extent as traditional students	Use it more than traditional students	Don't really keep track of this
Entire Sample	10.71%	21.43%	5.95%	61.90%

Table 1.16:   Use of Virtual Reference Services by Distance Learners vs. Traditional Students, Broken Out by U.S. and Non-U.S. Libraries

U.S. and Non-U.S. Libraries	Use the service less than traditional students	Use it about the same extent as traditional students	Use it more than traditional students	Don't really keep track of this
U.S.	10.45%	22.39%	5.97%	61.19%
Non-U.S.	11.76%	17.65%	5.88%	64.71%

Table 1.17:   Use of Virtual Reference Services by Distance Learners vs. Traditional Students, Broken Out by Carnegie Class

Carnegie Class	Use the service less than traditional students	Use it about the same extent as traditional students	Use it more than traditional students	Don't really keep track of this
Community College	10.71%	28.57%	0.00%	60.71%
4-Year Degree Granting College	16.67%	50.00%	0.00%	33.33%
MA or PhD Granting College	10.34%	13.79%	6.90%	68.97%
Research University	9.52%	14.29%	14.29%	61.90%

Table 1.18: Use of Virtual Reference Services by Distance Learners vs. Traditional Students, Broken Out by Public or Private Status

Public or Private Status	Use the service less than traditional students	Use it about the same extent as traditional students	Use it more than traditional students	Don't really keep track of this
Public College	9.38%	21.88%	4.69%	64.06%
Private College	15.00%	20.00%	10.00%	55.00%

Table 1.19: Use of Virtual Reference Services by Distance Learners vs. Traditional Students, Broken Out by Number of FTE Students at the Institution

Number of FTE Students at the Institution	Use the service less than traditional students	Use it about the same extent as traditional students	Use it more than traditional students	Don't really keep track of this
>12,000	9.52%	28.57%	9.52%	52.38%
6,001-12,000	5.00%	25.00%	10.00%	60.00%
2,500-6,000	19.05%	14.29%	4.76%	61.90%
<2,500	9.09%	18.18%	0.00%	72.73%

Table 1.20: Use of Virtual Reference Services by Distance Learners vs. Traditional Students, Broken Out by Number of FTE Distance Learners

Number of FTE Distance Learners	Use the service less than traditional students	Use it about the same extent as traditional students	Use it more than traditional students	Don't really keep track of this
>2,000	6.25%	31.25%	12.50%	50.00%
1,000-2,000	11.11%	16.67%	5.56%	66.67%
250-999	5.56%	22.22%	5.56%	66.67%
<250	6.25%	31.25%	6.25%	56.25%

Table 1.21: Use of Virtual Reference Services by Distance Learners vs. Traditional Students, Broken Out by Percentage of Distance Learners Living More than 50 Miles from Campus

Percentage of Distance Learners Living More than 50 Miles from Campus	Use the service less than traditional students	Use it about the same extent as traditional students	Use it more than traditional students	Don't really keep track of this
80-100%	16.67%	27.78%	11.11%	44.44%
51-79%	11.76%	23.53%	11.76%	52.94%
25-50%	5.00%	20.00%	5.00%	70.00%
1-24%	5.56%	27.78%	0.00%	66.67%

Chapter Two: Information Literacy Training for Distance Learners

Exactly half of survey respondents offered special classes or training programs for distance learners. Non-U.S. libraries were 20% more likely than U.S. libraries to offer such classes. Research universities were over twice as likely as community colleges to offer such programs. Just over 37% of four-year degree-granting colleges and 48% of MA or PhD-granting colleges offered such classes, while research universities led the way, with almost 82% offering the classes. Public colleges were just slightly more likely than private colleges to offer special classes for distance learners.

Just over 38% of institutions with fewer than 250 FTE distance learners offered info literacy training for distance learners, compared with 35% of institutions with between 250 and 999 FTE distance learners, more than 63% of institutions with between 1,000 and 2,000 FTE distance learners, and almost 56% of institutions with over 2,000 FTE distance learners.

Just over a third of the sample, 37%, offered any kind of formal non-credit or credit course worth 1, 2, or 3 credits on the subject of information literacy for either distance learners or traditional students. Research universities were the least likely to offer such courses, with just 27% reporting that they currently do this. By comparison, 31% of MA or PhD-granting colleges, half of four-year degree-granting colleges, and 47% of community colleges offered information literacy courses. Institutions with mid-sized enrollments, between 2,500 and 12,000 FTE students, were more likely to offer such courses, compared to other institutions.

Mid-sized colleges were roughly twice as likely as colleges with more than 12,000 students to offer information science courses. Colleges with the smallest enrollments, below 2,500, were in between the mid-sized and large enrollment colleges, with just a third of those colleges offering such classes. Information literacy classes were common among institutions with between 1,000 and 2,000 FTE distance learners, with over 68% of these institutions offering such courses. However, fewer than 39% of institutions with more than 2,000 or less than 1,000 FTE distance learners reported the same. The lowest percentage, just over 28%, was reported by institutions with fewer than 250 FTE distance learners. There was no clear correlation between percentage of distance learners living more than 50 miles away from campus and the availability of formal information literacy courses: While almost half of institutions with between 25 and 50% of their distance learners consisting of students living more than 50 miles away offered these courses, as few as 29% of institutions in the next tier, with between 51 and 79% of their distance learners living more than 50 miles away, reported the same. Institutions with either over 80% or under 24% of their distance learners coming from more than 50 miles away reported roughly the same incidences of these courses.

Just a quarter of our sample offered any kind of 0, 1, 2, or 3 credit course on information literacy, online or otherwise at a distance. There was no significant difference between U.S. and non-U.S. institutions in this regard. Four-year degree-granting colleges, at 37.5%, were more like than the other institution types to offer such a course. Just 20% of community colleges offered this course, while a quarter of MA and PhD-granting colleges and 28% of research universities did the same. Private colleges were 50% more likely than public colleges to offer information literacy courses online or at a distance. Institutions with between 2,500 and 6,000 FTE students were also 50% more likely than larger institutions to offer this type of course, while 29% of institutions with enrollments smaller than 2,500 FTE students reported the same. Mirroring the data we gathered on information literacy courses offered to distance learners and traditional students alike, institutions with between 1,000 and 2,000 FTE distance learning students reported far higher availability of information literacy courses offered online or otherwise at a distance. As few as 14% of institutions with fewer than 250 FTE distance learners offered such a course. There was no clear correlation between percentage of distance learning students who lived more than 50 miles away from campus and the availability of this course, as the numbers varied greatly. Roughly a third of institutions with more than 80% or between 25 and 50% of their distance learners living more than 50 miles away offered this course, compared to under 6% of institutions whose distance learners consisted of between 51 and 79% students who lived more than 50 miles away, and 15% of institutions whose distance learners comprised under 24% of their distance learners.

Among libraries that did not, at the time of our survey, offer any courses in information literacy online, over a third had no plans to introduce such a course within the next two years. Just under 29% reported that they had plans to introduce such a course within the next two years, while almost 37% reported that they had no such plans for the next two years, but that it was a possibility for later on. In this regard, 40% of non-U.S. libraries had such a course planned for the next two years, compared to just 26% of U.S. libraries. U.S. libraries were, however, slightly more optimistic about adding such a course in the more distant future, compared to non-U.S. libraries, with 37.7% and 33% reporting, respectively. Four-year degree granting colleges led the way, with the higher percentage reporting to already have plans for such a course to be introduced in the next two years. Community colleges came in close, at 37%, while just under 30% of MA or PhD-granting colleges and 12% of research universities had such plans already in the works. Research universities differed from MA or PhD-granting colleges in that almost half of the research universities responded that the possibility existed for having a program in the more distant future, compared to almost 30% of MA or PhD-granting colleges. Public colleges were almost twice as likely as private colleges to have plans to introduce an online information literacy course within the next two years, but were just as likely as private colleges to think that such a course might be developed in more than two years. Half of the institutions with between 2,500 and 6,000 FTE students responded that they had plans to introduce such a course within the next 2 years. By comparison, under 12% of institutions with fewer than 2,500 FTE students, 20% of institutions with between 6,001 and 12,000 FTE students, and a third of institutions with over 12,000 FTE students reported the same. Institutions with the smallest enrollments, however, were more hopeful about instituting such a course after two years than institutions of other sizes. More than a third of institutions with between 250 and 2,000 FTE distance learning students already had an online information literacy course to be introduced in the next two years. By comparison, just 11% of institutions with fewer than 250 FTE distance learners and 21% of institutions with more than 2,000 FTE distance learners reported the same. As the proportion of distance learning students living more than 50 miles away increased, so did the likelihood that the institution did not have plans to create an online information literacy course in the next two years. However, for those institutions with plans to introduce an online information literacy course within the next two years, the proportion of distance learners living further than 50 miles away was not a very good indicator: Anywhere between 25% and 33% of the four tiers of colleges with students living more than 50 miles away comprising a certain amount of their distance learners reported plans to introduce an online information literacy course in the next two years.

The majority of the sample, over 72%, had a Web page on the library Website dedicated to the needs of distance learners. There was no significant difference between data reported by U.S. and non-U.S. libraries, nor between public colleges and private colleges. Almost 91% of research libraries had such a Web page, compared to 77% of MA or PhD-granting colleges, 75% of four-year degree granting colleges, and just under 56% of community colleges. Eight out of 10 institutions with over 12,000 FTE students had a Web page catering to distance learners' needs, while roughly 70% of colleges with smaller enrollments reported the same. In general, as the number of FTE distance learners increased, so did the incidence of Web pages dedicated to distance learners. There was a steep difference between institutions with over 1,000 FTE distance learners, almost 90% of which had such a Web page, and those with under 1,000 FTE distance learning students. Just 57% of respondents with fewer than 250 FTE distance learners and 65% of respondents with between 250 and 999 FTE distance learners reported the same. About seven out of 10 institutions with either very high or very low percentages of distance learners living more than 50 miles away, above 80 or below 25% had such a Web page, while over 82% of institutions whose distance learners living more than 50 miles away comprised between 25 and 79% of their distance learners reported the same.

Few respondents maintained a blog or listserv catering specifically to the needs of distance learners. Only one in 10 had such a blog or listserv, with non-U.S. libraries reporting almost 3 times as much as U.S. libraries. While between 12 and 14% of colleges granting four-year degrees, MAs or PhDs, and research universities had a blog or listserv for distance learners, just below 3% of community colleges reported the same. There was almost no difference in the data reported by private and public colleges, though private colleges were slightly ahead of public ones. Sixteen percent of institutions with particularly high FTE enrollments, those above 12,000, had a blog or listserv for their distance learners, and 12% of institutions with between 2,500 and 6,000 FTE students reported the same, both being above the sample average. However, just over 8% of institutions with fewer than 2,500 FTE students had such a blog or listserv, and just 4% of institutions with between 6,001 and 12,000 students reported the same. Not surprisingly, the incidence of a blog or listserv for distance learners increased as the number of FTE distance learners increased. In fact, no college with under 250 FTE distance learners indicated they had such a blog or listserv, while 10% of institutions with between 250 and 999 FTE distance learners, 21% of those with between 1,000 and 2,000 FTE distance learners, and almost 17% of those with over 2,000 FTE distance learners reported the same. Similarly, no colleges with fewer than 25% of their distance learners living more than 50 miles away had a blog or listserv for distance learners. However, the highest incidence of a distance learning blog or listserv was reported by the tier of institutions with between 51 and 79% of their distance learners living more than 50 miles away. By comparison, 13% of institutions with more than 80% of their distance learners living more than 50 miles away and just over 4% of institutions with 25 to 50% of their distance learners living more than 50 miles away reported the same.

The mean number of interactive online tutorials explaining various facets of the library to patrons was 6.16, with a median of 0. The maximum number reported was 100.

Survey of Library Services for Distance Learning Programs

Private colleges reported almost 3 times the mean number of interactive online tutorials as public colleges, as well as 3 times the median. Institutions with over 12,000 reported a mean of 6.76 and median of 3, while those with fewer than 2,500 FTE students reported a mean of 9.55 and median of 3.5. Institutions with between 2,500 and 6,000 FTE students reported a mean of 5.17 tutorials, but a median of 1.5. The data according to the number of FTE distance learners reflects that data gathered according to number of FTE students. Those colleges with the smallest number of FTE distance learners reported a mean of 9.85 and median of 3.5, while those with over 1,000 FTE distance learners reported over 6.5 mean tutorials. Those with between 250 and 999 FTE distance learners reported just 3.95 mean tutorials, however, and a median of 2.5. The most tutorials offered by a library, according to the percentage of their distance learning students who live more than 50 miles away, was by the colleges with fewer than a quarter of them living more than 50 miles away. Those whose distance learners living more than 50 miles away comprised between 25 to 50% of their distance learning students reported a mean of just 3.43 and median of 1. Institutions whose distance learners living more than 50 miles away comprised more than 80% reported a mean number of online interactive tutorials of 5.64 and median of 4.

Seven in 10 respondents did not keep track of distance learners' usage of library-sponsored, posted or directed tutorials and guides to the library's resources, compared to traditional students. Over 14% reported that distance learners and traditional students used these tutorials and guides to the same extent, while over 11% reported that distance learners actually used these resources more than traditional students. Just over 4% of respondents indicated that their distance learners used these resources less than traditional students did. Non-U.S. libraries appeared to keep track of these statistics more than U.S. libraries: 73% of U.S. libraries reported not to have a good idea of this, compared to just 58% of non-U.S. libraries. Twice as many non-U.S. libraries reported that distance learners and traditional students used the tutorials and guides to the same extent, while answers that distance learners used such resource either more or less than traditional students remained within just a few percent of each other. Among various Carnegie classes of institutions we surveyed, no four-year degree-granting colleges reported that their distance learners used these resources more than traditional students, while as many as 20% of MA or PhD-granting colleges reported the same. Community colleges and research universities were in between, with 6 and 9%, respectively. Four-year degree-granting colleges, in fact, were more likely than any of the other institution types to report that their distance learners used these resources less than traditional students did, more than doubling the community colleges' rate, 6%, and nearly tripling the research universities', at just over 4%. No MA or PhD-granting college reported that their distance learners used the library-sponsored tutorials and guides less than their traditional students. Public colleges reported over double the rate at which their distance learners and traditional students used these resources to the same extent, 17% to 8%. Private colleges, however, were 60% more likely to report that their distance learners used such resources more than traditional students. And while under 6% of public colleges reported that their distance learners used these resources less than traditional students did, no private college reported the same. Institutions with over 12,000 or under 2,500 FTE students reported similar numbers, between 12.5 and 13% of them indicating that distance learners and traditional students used these resources to the same extent. Mid-sized institutions, with FTE enrollments between 2,500 and 12,000, reported the same numbers as well, with 16% of them reporting the same. However, smaller institutions, with fewer than 6,000 FTE students, were up to twice as likely to report that their distance learners used such tutorials and guides more than traditional students. Just 8% of the institutions with over 6,000 FTE students reported distance learners' higher usage, compared to traditional students. Institutions with between 1,000 and 2,000 FTE distance learners were most likely to report the same usage by distance learners and traditional students, while just under 6% of institutions with over 2,000 FTE distance learners reported the same. Institutions with fewer distance learners were in between; almost 16% of those with between 250 and 999 FTE distance learners and 14% of those with fewer than 250 FTE distance learners reported the same. As the number of FTE distance learners decreased, institutions appeared more likely to indicate that their distance learners used these tutorials and guides more than traditional students. Similarly, as the number of FTE distance learners increased, so did institutions begin indicating that their distance learners used these resources less than traditional students. This would indicate that the resources are better used by distance learners, or at least are used more than by the traditional students, when there were fewer than 1,000 FTE distance learners at that institution. Roughly a quarter of the institutions with more than half of their distance learners living more than 50 miles away reported that their distance learners and traditional students used their online guides and tutorials to the same extent, compared to 13% of institutions with between 25 and 50% of their distance learners living more than 50 miles away and 0% of institutions with fewer than 25% of their distance learners living more than 50 miles away. However, just over 17% of institutions with over 80% or between 25 and 50% of their distance learners living more than 50 miles away indicated that their distance learners used these resources more than traditional students. Institutions with between 51 and 79% of their distance learners reported that almost 6% of them thought that their distance learners' usage was higher than that of their traditional students', while just 10.5% of the institutions with fewer than 25% of their distance learners living more than 50 miles away reported the same.

When participants were asked to share what measures they have taken to accommodate distance learning students, we learned that many focused on virtual offerings: dedicated Web content for distance learners, including video and text tutorials, guides and help pages tailored specifically for distance learners, email reference and live chat services, blogs, document delivery of electronic materials, and specific contact information for distance learners. Many mentioned specifically putting links to these resources in their course management software and library Web pages. With remote users and distance learners in mind, several have increased their attention to remote accessability, setting up proxy servers, and increasing subscriptions to full-text articles and Web versions of journals. Several respondents mentioned having a toll-free number for students to call, as well as offering video conferencing and in-person instruction, wherein the librarian visits the students on-site. One participant mentioned offering research services in the case where the student has no access. Physical brochures, extended loan periods, library guides on CD, and library-conducted surveys aimed at distance learners were also mentioned.

Table 2.1:   Percentage of Libraries that Offer Special Classes or Training Programs for Distance Learners

	Yes	No
Entire Sample	50.00%	50.00%

Table 2.2: Percentage of Libraries that Offer Special Classes or Training Programs for Distance Learners, Broken Out by U.S. and Non-U.S. Libraries

U.S. and Non-U.S. Libraries	Yes	No
U.S.	48.10%	51.90%
Non-U.S.	57.89%	42.11%

Table 2.3: Percentage of Libraries that Offer Special Classes or Training Programs for Distance Learners, Broken Out by Carnegie Class

Carnegie Class	Yes	No
Community College	33.33%	66.67%
4-Year Degree Granting College	37.50%	62.50%
MA or PhD Granting College	48.57%	51.43%
Research University	81.82%	18.18%

Table 2.4: Percentage of Libraries that Offer Special Classes or Training Programs for Distance Learners, Broken Out by Public or Private Status

Public or Private Status	Yes	No
Public College	51.39%	48.61%
Private College	46.15%	53.85%

Table 2.5: Percentage of Libraries that Offer Special Classes or Training Programs for Distance Learners, Broken Out by Number of FTE Students at the Institution

Number of FTE Students at the Institution	Yes	No
>12,000	50.00%	50.00%
6,001-12,000	52.00%	48.00%
2,500-6,000	52.00%	48.00%
<2500	45.83%	54.17%

Table 2.6: Percentage of Libraries that Offer Special Classes or Training Programs for Distance Learners, Broken Out by Number of FTE Distance Learners

Number of FTE Distance Learners	Yes	No
>2,000	55.56%	44.44%
1,000-2,000	63.16%	36.84%
250-999	35.00%	65.00%
<250	38.10%	61.90%

Table 2.7:   Percentage of Libraries that Offer Special Classes or Training Programs for Distance Learners, Broken Out by Percentage of Distance Learners Living More than 50 Miles from Campus

Percentage of Distance Learners Living More than 50 Miles from Campus	Yes	No
80-100%	65.22%	34.78%
51-79%	52.94%	47.06%
25-50%	47.83%	52.17%
1-24%	40.00%	60.00%

Table 2.8:   Percentage of Libraries that Offer Any Formal Kind of 0-3 Credit Course in Information Literacy for Either Distance Learners or Traditional Students

	Yes	No
Entire Sample	37.37%	62.63%

Table 2.9:   Percentage of Libraries that Offer Any Formal Kind of 0-3 Credit Course in Information Literacy for Either Distance Learners or Traditional Students, Broken Out by U.S. and Non-U.S. Libraries

U.S. and Non-U.S. Libraries	Yes	No
U.S.	37.50%	62.50%
Non-U.S.	36.84%	63.16%

Table 2.10:   Percentage of Libraries that Offer Any Formal Kind of 0-3 Credit Course in Information Literacy for Either Distance Learners or Traditional Students, Broken Out by Carnegie Class

Carnegie Class	Yes	No
Community College	47.06%	52.94%
4-Year Degree Granting College	50.00%	50.00%
MA or PhD Granting College	31.43%	68.57%
Research University	27.27%	72.73%

Table 2.11:   Percentage of Libraries that Offer Any Formal Kind of 0-3 Credit Course in Information Literacy for Either Distance Learners or Traditional Students, Broken Out by Public or Private Status

Public or Private Status	Yes	No
Public College	36.99%	63.01%
Private College	38.46%	61.54%

Table 2.12:   Percentage of Libraries that Offer Any Formal Kind of 0-3 Credit Course in Information Literacy for Either Distance Learners or Traditional Students, Broken Out by Number of FTE Students at the Institution

Number of FTE Students at the Institution	Yes	No
>12,000	24.00%	76.00%
6,001-1,2000	44.00%	56.00%
2,500-6,000	48.00%	52.00%
<2500	33.33%	66.67%

Table 2.13:   Percentage of Libraries that Offer Any Formal Kind of 0-3 Credit Course in Information Literacy for Either for Distance Learners or Traditional Students, Broken Out by Number of FTE Distance Learners

Number of FTE Distance Learners	Yes	No
>2,000	38.89%	61.11%
1,000-2,000	68.42%	31.58%
250-999	35.00%	65.00%
<250	28.57%	71.43%

Table 2.14:   Percentage of Libraries that Offer Any Formal Kind of 0-3 Credit Course in Information Literacy for Either for Distance Learners or Traditional Students, Broken Out by Percentage of Distance Learners Living More than 50 Miles from Campus

Percentage of Distance Learners Living More than 50 Miles from Campus	Yes	No
80-100%	34.78%	65.22%
51-79%	29.41%	70.59%
25-50%	47.83%	52.17%
1-24%	35.00%	65.00%

Table 2.15:   Percentage of Libraries that Offer Any Kind of 0-3 Credit Online or Other Course at a Distance in Information Literacy

	Yes	No
Entire Sample	25.51%	74.49%

Table 2.16:   Percentage of Libraries that Offer Any Kind of 0-3 Credit Online or Other Course at a Distance in Information Literacy, Broken Out by U.S. and Non-U.S. Libraries

U.S. and Non-U.S. Libraries	Yes	No
U.S.	25.32%	74.68%
Non-U.S.	26.32%	73.68%

Table 2.17:   Percentage of Libraries that Offer Any Kind of 0-3 Credit Online or Other Course at a Distance in Information Literacy, Broken Out by Carnegie Class

Carnegie Class	Yes	No
Community College	20.59%	79.41%
4-Year Degree Granting College	37.50%	62.50%
MA or PhD Granting College	25.71%	74.29%
Research University	28.57%	71.43%

Table 2.18:   Percentage of Libraries that Offer Any Kind of 0-3 Credit Online or Other Course at a Distance in Information Literacy, Broken Out by Public or Private Status

Public or Private Status	Yes	No
Public College	22.22%	77.78%
Private College	34.62%	65.38%

Table 2.19:   Percentage of Libraries that Offer Any Kind of 0-3 Credit Online or Other Course at a Distance in Information Literacy, Broken Out by Number of FTE Students at the Institution

Number of FTE Students at the Institution	Yes	No
>12,000	20.00%	80.00%
6,001-12,000	20.00%	80.00%
2,500-6,000	33.33%	66.67%
<2500	29.17%	70.83%

Table 2.20:   Percentage of Libraries that Offer Any Kind of 0-3 Credit Online or Other Course at a Distance in Information Literacy, Broken Out by Number of FTE Distance Learners

Number of FTE Distance Learners	Yes	No
>2,000	22.22%	77.78%
1,000-2,000	57.89%	42.11%
250-999	20.00%	80.00%
<250	14.29%	85.71%

Table 2.21:   Percentage of Libraries that Offer Any Kind of 0-3 Credit Online or Other Course at a Distance in Information Literacy, Broken Out by Percentage of Distance Learners Living More than 50 Miles from Campus

Percentage of Distance Learners Living More than 50 Miles from Campus	Yes	No
80-100%	36.36%	63.64%
51-79%	5.88%	94.12%
25-50%	30.43%	69.57%
1-24%	15.00%	85.00%

Table 2.22:   Future Plans of Libraries that Do Not Offer Any Online Information Literacy Courses

	Have no plans to introduce one within the next two years	Have plans to introduce one within the next two years	Probably will not introduce one within the next two years but possibly later on
Entire Sample	34.21%	28.95%	36.84%

Table 2.23:   Future Plans of Libraries that Do Not Offer Any Online Information Literacy Courses, Broken Out by U.S. and Non-U.S. Libraries

U.S. and Non-U.S. Libraries	Have no plans to introduce one within the next two years	Have plans to introduce one within the next two years	Probably will not introduce one within the next two years but possibly later on
U.S.	36.07%	26.23%	37.70%
Non-U.S.	26.67%	40.00%	33.33%

Table 2.24:   Future Plans of Libraries that Do Not Offer Any Online Information Literacy Courses, Broken Out by Carnegie Class

Carnegie Class	Have no plans to introduce one within the next two years	Have plans to introduce one within the next two years	Probably will not introduce one within the next two years but possibly later on
Community College	25.93%	37.04%	37.04%
4-Year Degree Granting College	20.00%	40.00%	40.00%
MA or PhD Granting College	40.74%	29.63%	29.63%
Research University	41.18%	11.76%	47.06%

Table 2.25: Future Plans of Libraries that Do Not Offer Any Online Information Literacy Courses, Broken Out by Public or Private Status

Public or Private Status	Have no plans to introduce one within the next two years	Have plans to introduce one within the next two years	Probably will not introduce one within the next two years but possibly later on
Public College	30.51%	32.20%	37.29%
Private College	47.06%	17.65%	35.29%

Table 2.26: Future Plans of Libraries that Do Not Offer Any Online Information Literacy Courses, Broken Out by Number of FTE Students at the Institution

Number of FTE Students at the Institution	Have no plans to introduce one within the next two years	Have plans to introduce one within the next two years	Probably will not introduce one within the next two years but possibly later on
>12,000	42.86%	33.33%	23.81%
6,001-12,000	40.00%	20.00%	40.00%
2,500-6,000	16.67%	50.00%	33.33%
<2500	35.29%	11.76%	52.94%

Table 2.27: Future Plans of Libraries that Do Not Offer Any Online Information Literacy Courses, Broken Out by Number of FTE Distance Learners

Number of FTE Distance Learners	Have no plans to introduce one within the next two years	Have plans to introduce one within the next two years	Probably will not introduce one within the next two years but possibly later on
>2,000	42.86%	21.43%	35.71%
1,000-2,000	37.50%	37.50%	25.00%
250-999	27.78%	33.33%	38.89%
<250	44.44%	11.11%	44.44%

Table 2.28: Future Plans of Libraries that Do Not Offer Any Online Information Literacy Courses, Broken Out by Percentage of Distance Learners Living More than 50 Miles from Campus

Percentage of Distance Learners Living More than 50 Miles from Campus	Have no plans to introduce one within the next two years	Have plans to introduce one within the next two years	Probably will not introduce one within the next two years but possibly later on
80-100%	42.86%	28.57%	28.57%
51-79%	31.25%	25.00%	43.75%
25-50%	27.78%	33.33%	38.89%
1-24%	29.41%	29.41%	41.18%

Table 2.29: Percentage of Libraries that have a Web Page on the Library Website Specifically Catering to the Needs of Distance Learners

	Yes	No
Entire Sample	72.73%	27.27%

Table 2.30: Percentage of Libraries that have a Web Page on the Library Website Specifically Catering to the Needs of Distance Learners, Broken Out by U.S. and Non-U.S. Libraries

U.S. and Non-U.S. Libraries	Yes	No
U.S.	72.50%	27.50%
Non-U.S.	73.68%	26.32%

Table 2.31: Percentage of Libraries that have a Web Page on the Library Website Specifically Catering to the Needs of Distance Learners, Broken Out by Carnegie Class

Carnegie Class	Yes	No
Community College	55.88%	44.12%
4-Year Degree Granting College	75.00%	25.00%
MA or PhD Granting College	77.14%	22.86%
Research University	90.91%	9.09%

Table 2.32: Percentage of Libraries that have a Web Page on the Library Website Specifically Catering to the Needs of Distance Learners, Broken Out by Public or Private Status

Public or Private Status	Yes	No
Public College	72.60%	27.40%
Private College	73.08%	26.92%

Table 2.33: Percentage of Libraries that have a Web Page on the Library Website Specifically Catering to the Needs of Distance Learners, Broken Out by Number of FTE Students at the Institution

Number of FTE Students at the Institution	Yes	No
>12,000	80.00%	20.00%
6,001-12,000	68.00%	32.00%
2,500-6,000	72.00%	28.00%
<2,500	70.83%	29.17%

Table 2.34: Percentage of Libraries that have a Web Page on the Library Website Specifically Catering to the Needs of Distance Learners, Broken Out by Number of FTE Distance Learners

Number of FTE Distance Learners	Yes	No
>2,000	88.89%	11.11%
1,000-2,000	89.47%	10.53%
250-999	65.00%	35.00%
<250	57.14%	42.86%

Table 2.35: Percentage of Libraries that have a Web Page on the Library Website Specifically Catering to the Needs of Distance Learners, Broken Out by Percentage of Distance Learners Living More than 50 Miles from Campus

Percentage of Distance Learners Living More than 50 Miles from Campus	Yes	No
80-100%	69.57%	30.43%
51-79%	82.35%	17.65%
25-50%	82.61%	17.39%
1-24%	70.00%	30.00%

Table 2.36: Percentage of Libraries that have a Blog or Listserv Specifically Catering to the Needs of Distance Learners

	Yes	No
Entire Sample	10.10%	89.90%

Table 2.37: Percentage of Libraries that have a Blog or Listserv Specifically Catering to the Needs of Distance Learners, Broken Out by U.S. and Non-U.S. Libraries

U.S. and Non-U.S. Libraries	Yes	No
U.S.	7.50%	92.50%
Non-U.S.	21.05%	78.95%

Table 2.38: Percentage of Libraries that have a Blog or Listserv Specifically Catering to the Needs of Distance Learners, Broken Out by Carnegie Class

Carnegie Class	Yes	No
Community College	2.94%	97.06%
4-Year Degree Granting College	12.50%	87.50%
MA or PhD Granting College	14.29%	85.71%
Research University	13.64%	86.36%

Table 2.39: Percentage of Libraries that have a Blog or Listserv Specifically Catering to the Needs of Distance Learners, Broken Out by Public or Private Status

Public or Private Status	Yes	No
Public College	9.59%	90.41%
Private College	11.54%	88.46%

Table 2.40: Percentage of Libraries that have a Blog or Listserv Specifically Catering to the Needs of Distance Learners, Broken Out by Number of FTE Students at the Institution

Number of FTE Students at the Institution	Yes	No
>12,000	16.00%	84.00%
6,001-12,000	4.00%	96.00%
2,500-6,000	12.00%	88.00%
<2,500	8.33%	91.67%

Table 2.41: Percentage of Libraries that have a Blog or Listserv Specifically Catering to the Needs of Distance Learners, Broken Out by Number of FTE Distance Learners

Number of FTE Distance Learners	Yes	No
>2,000	16.67%	83.33%
1,000-2,000	21.05%	78.95%
250-999	10.00%	90.00%
<250	0.00%	100.00%

Table 2.42: Percentage of Libraries that have a Blog or Listserv Specifically Catering to the Needs of Distance Learners, Broken Out by Percentage of Distance Learners Living More than 50 Miles from Campus

Percentage of Distance Learners Living More than 50 Miles from Campus	Yes	No
80-100%	13.04%	86.96%
51-79%	23.53%	76.47%
25-50%	4.35%	95.65%
1-24%	0.00%	100.00%

Table 2.43:   Mean, Median, Minimum and Maximum Number of Interactive Online Tutorials Explaining Various Facets of the Library to Patrons

	Mean	Median	Minimum	Maximum
Entire Sample	6.16	3.00	0.00	100.00

Table 2.44:   Mean, Median, Minimum and Maximum Number of Interactive Online Tutorials Explaining Various Facets of the Library to Patrons, Broken Out by U.S. and Non-U.S. Libraries

U.S. and Non-U.S. Libraries	Mean	Median	Minimum	Maximum
U.S.	6.43	3.00	0.00	100.00
Non-U.S.	5.05	3.00	0.00	20.00

Table 2.45:   Mean, Median, Minimum and Maximum Number of Interactive Online Tutorials Explaining Various Facets of the Library to Patrons, Broken Out by Carnegie Class

Carnegie Class	Mean	Median	Minimum	Maximum
Community College	2.76	0.00	0.00	25.00
4-Year Degree Granting College	3.88	4.50	0.00	10.00
MA or PhD Granting College	10.56	5.00	0.00	100.00
Research University	5.82	3.50	0.00	21.00

Table 2.46:   Mean, Median, Minimum and Maximum Number of Interactive Online Tutorials Explaining Various Facets of the Library to Patrons, Broken Out by Public or Private Status

Public or Private Status	Mean	Median	Minimum	Maximum
Public College	4.17	2.00	0.00	25.00
Private College	11.80	6.00	0.00	100.00

Table 2.47: Mean, Median, Minimum and Maximum Number of Interactive Online Tutorials Explaining Various Facets of the Library to Patrons, Broken Out by Number of FTE Students at the Institution

Number of FTE Students at the Institution	Mean	Median	Minimum	Maximum
>12,000	6.76	3.00	0.00	36.00
6,001-12,000	3.52	3.00	0.00	20.00
2,500-6,000	5.17	1.50	0.00	22.00
<2,500	9.55	3.50	0.00	100.00

Table 2.48: Mean, Median, Minimum and Maximum Number of Interactive Online Tutorials Explaining Various Facets of the Library to Patrons, Broken Out by Number of FTE Distance Learners

Number of FTE Distance Learners	Mean	Median	Minimum	Maximum
>2,000	6.78	3.50	0.00	25.00
1,000-2,000	6.58	3.00	0.00	22.00
250-999	3.95	2.50	0.00	15.00
<250	9.85	3.50	0.00	100.00

Table 2.49: Mean, Median, Minimum and Maximum Number of Interactive Online Tutorials Explaining Various Facets of the Library to Patrons, Broken Out by Percentage of Distance Learners Living More than 50 Miles from Campus

Percentage of Distance Learners Living More than 50 Miles from Campus	Mean	Median	Minimum	Maximum
80-100%	5.64	4.00	0.00	20.00
51-79%	7.38	5.50	0.00	21.00
25-50%	3.43	1.00	0.00	15.00
1-24%	9.80	1.50	0.00	100.00

Table 2.50: Use of Library Sponsored, Posted or Directed Tutorials and Guides to the Library's Resources by Distance Learners vs. Traditional Students

	About the same extent as traditional students	More than traditional students use them	Less than traditional students use them	We don't really have a good idea of this
Entire Sample	14.43%	11.34%	4.12%	70.10%

Table 2.51: Use of Library Sponsored, Posted or Directed Tutorials and Guides to the Library's Resources by Distance Learners vs. Traditional Students, Broken Out by U.S. and Non-U.S. Libraries

U.S. and Non-U.S. Libraries	About the same extent as traditional students	More than traditional students use them	Less than traditional students use them	We don't really have a good idea of this
U.S.	11.54%	11.54%	3.85%	73.08%
Non-U.S.	26.32%	10.53%	5.26%	57.89%

Table 2.52: Use of Library Sponsored, Posted or Directed Tutorials and Guides to the Library's Resources by Distance Learners vs. Traditional Students, Broken Out by Carnegie Class

Carnegie Class	About the same extent as traditional students	More than traditional students use them	Less than traditional students use them	We don't really have a good idea of this
Community College	15.15%	6.06%	6.06%	72.73%
4-Year Degree Granting College	14.29%	0.00%	14.29%	71.43%
MA or PhD Granting College	14.29%	20.00%	0.00%	65.71%
Research University	13.64%	9.09%	4.55%	72.73%

Table 2.53: Use of Library Sponsored, Posted or Directed Tutorials and Guides to the Library's Resources by Distance Learners vs. Traditional Students, Broken Out by Public or Private Status

Public or Private Status	About the same extent as traditional students	More than traditional students use them	Less than traditional students use them	We don't really have a good idea of this
Public College	16.90%	9.86%	5.63%	67.61%
Private College	7.69%	15.38%	0.00%	76.92%

Table 2.54:   Use of Library Sponsored, Posted or Directed Tutorials and Guides to the Library's Resources by Distance Learners vs. Traditional Students, Broken Out by Number of FTE Students at the Institution

Number of FTE Students at the Institution	About the same extent as traditional students	More than traditional students use them	Less than traditional students use them	We don't really have a good idea of this
>12,000	13.04%	8.70%	0.00%	78.26%
6,001-12,000	16.00%	8.00%	12.00%	64.00%
2,500-6,000	16.00%	16.00%	0.00%	68.00%
<2,500	12.50%	12.50%	4.17%	70.83%

Table 2.55:   Use of Library Sponsored, Posted or Directed Tutorials and Guides to the Library's Resources by Distance Learners vs. Traditional Students, Broken Out by Number of FTE Distance Learners

Number of FTE Distance Learners	About the same extent as traditional students	More than traditional students use them	Less than traditional students use them	We don't really have a good idea of this
>2,000	5.88%	5.88%	11.76%	76.47%
1,000-2,000	21.05%	10.53%	10.53%	57.89%
250-999	15.79%	15.79%	0.00%	68.42%
<250	14.29%	19.05%	0.00%	66.67%

Table 2.56:   Use of Library Sponsored, Posted or Directed Tutorials and Guides to the Library's Resources by Distance Learners vs. Traditional Students, Broken Out by Percentage of Distance Learners Living More than 50 Miles from Campus

Percentage of Distance Learners Living More than 50 Miles from Campus	About the same extent as traditional students	More than traditional students use them	Less than traditional students use them	We don't really have a good idea of this
80-100%	26.09%	17.39%	4.35%	52.17%
51-79%	23.53%	5.88%	0.00%	70.59%
25-50%	13.04%	17.39%	0.00%	69.57%
1-24%	0.00%	10.53%	5.26%	84.21%

Survey of Library Services for Distance Learning Programs

Answers to the prompt, "Please describe the measures that your library has taken to serve your college's distance learning students. Mention any practices, resources, technology or other facets of your trade that have helped you to serve distance learning students."

1. We have developed the distance learning tutorials, and have given out passwords to our databases to distance learning students

2. Library tab on all d/l course home pages, push content links to classes, online tutorials.

3. Distinctions here are blurred. Every faculty member is encouraged to use Blackboard to support their courses. Lots of use of technology to support learning. This has resulted in plenty of blended classes. There are only a few programs that provide complete programs "at a distance." I don't see a student headcount for "distance students" in any of the university's data. On the other hand, we've been acutely aware of remote users for many years. We have a toll-free in-state phone line. We have had email reference service since 1995. We also have real-time chat, though we have experienced little use. Our access services librarian has developed some methods for getting library ID numbers to students who might be on alternate schedules or "at a distance." The USF ID Center has established a method for students to recieve ID cards without coming to campus. Our reference department uses Elluminate to offer real-time instruction on the use of library resources to our remote users. Examples from this semester: We will be doing some "how to use the library" for courses offered in the College of Education and the School of Performing and Visual Arts. In some cases, librarians are able to travel to off-campus locations (usually at other USF campuses or nearby community colleges) to offer some instructional support. We offer some extended interlibrary loan services to students at no charge; mainly the library is willing to send articles we have in print in the building to distance learners as well as articles from other libraries around the country. (P.S. Another problem with the stats you requested: Many of our students taking face-to-face classes live more than 50 miles away from the Tampa campus. Very hard to estimate!)

4. Online tutorials, chat, email reference, photocopying services for a fee, electronic reserves.

5. Development of an Online Student Resources Webpage. Development of an online tutorial suite. Librarians actively embedded in some courses' LMS (Blackboard). Participation in 24/7 library chat cooperative.

6. We add library guides and useful Weblinks to the online courses in our college's course management system (ANGEL). We also offer document delivery of books and articles to our distance ed. students. We have also taken on an initiative of subscribing to more full-text databases.

7. I am still learning the position (have only been doing this for two months.) I would say that having 1.5 staff (+ 1 professional staff) has been extremely helpful with filling document delivery requests and serving the students. Of course, the Web, and having fulsome e-journal subscriptions as well as ebooks, has been a boon. Screen capture software and Camtasia-like products have really helped with instruction.

8. At the request of instructors, we will travel to off-campus meeting sites to deliver face-to-face library instruction as time and budget permits. There are links to downloadable PDF "practice guides" offering step-by-step library instruction. Our most used services are telephone and e-mail assistance. Most of our distant students are older and have full-time jobs and families. Many would rather not deal with too much technology.

9. We have a dedicated Web page as well as a array of online tutorials. We have a toll-free number. The library has a link on each WebCT course page.

10. Extended loan periods, access to other U.K.-based HE Libraries, access to local colleges. Access to e-resources and digitising restricted loan material.

11. Dedicated staff to provide library materials. Send library materials to students directly. Offer 1-800 phone service for student requests.

12. Allocated a librarian on a halftime basis to develop and provide services to online students.

13. Hired a DE librarian with zero budget allocated.

14. Remote Authentication for all databases, ebooks, and streaming video collections; 24/7 chat reference; online, open entry, self-paced 1 or 2 credit library skills classes.

15. We offer a postal loan service for books. For those DLs who have a summer school or introductory day, we offer intense information skills classes. We are bringing on an IM service in the next few weeks.

16. Posting books, dedicated enquiry service, extended loans, membership of reciprocal borrowing schemes.

17. Not a great deal other than one information literacy course in one graduate program, distance ed Web page, tutorials and Ask-a-Librarian venues.

18. We are currently working to develop online tutorials to educate DE students on the services we offer.

19. Work with faculty to incorporate online library use into assignments, offer online sessions as part of the class (by video or video conferencing), work with staff at other libraries which distance students use (joint degree programs), print handouts/pamphlets distributed to distance students.

20. The librarian with responsibility for DL students works with the faculty member teaching the course to integrate library guides into the course on Blackboard. The librarian also offers a Student/Librarian discussion forum in the course. Every DL student receives a student ID card (issued by the library) with an informational library brochure and a letter from the DL librarian explaining how to access our online resources and contact us when needed.

21. Access to library's databases and ebooks from any location; mail out books; videoconference library instruction session to campuses outside city; offer email Ask a Question service; offer Live Chat messaging; will conduct research if student has no access; prepare brochure specifically for students; have specific Web page for students; offer free long distance telephone reference service; offer online renewals.

22. We work with community liaison coordinators to arrange on-site library instruction sessions. Basically, I travel to do face-to-face instruction with them.

We also ensure that as many resource licenses as possible include off-campus access, and ensure seamless access using a proxy server.

23. Remote access to most of our electronic resources, library catalog, subject guides and tutoring materials. Mail out brochure to each distance student with a library card and instructions on how to activate it for remote access.

24. Library resources are mailed/faxed/emailed to them Additional electronic full-text resources have been purchased to support distance education. Proxy server and URL resolver installed. Special consideration is given to distance learning when they ask reference questions.

25. Librarians who serve as liaisons to academic departments find out what courses are offered via distance ed and on regional campuses and contact faculty to offer library instruction. Our university uses the Blackboard course management system, and librarians offer links to online tutorials and guides to professors to integrate into classes. We began using LibGuides from Springshare in fall 2007, and these are accessible to distance ed students and faculty and very flexible to customize for specific classes and/or assignments. For IM reference we use Meebo because it's platform nonspecific; email reference appears to be more used by distance ed students, though we don't have a way to track the sources of IM sessions except by asking specifically, which we don't always remember to do.

26. Information literacy modules included in a few online courses; librarian travels to satellite campuses for classroom instruction.

27. Virtual reference tools (email and IM), increased ILL & doc del services, phone support and integration of library resources into course management software (Blackboard Vista & Blackboard).

28. Onsite instruction; Web-based tutorials; presentations through Camtasia and interactive video; CD-ROM tutorials.

29. We've yet to do this. However, it is one of our objectives for 2008.

30. We have recently added a proxy server. We seek journals and reference books that are Web-based. We look for online databases that benefit the most students. Our library feels that services (Web page, email, reference, databases etc) benefit all students no matter where they are located.

31. This is really new and under development for us. We are starting to mail out materials.

32. We try to subscribe to the online versions of journals in the disciplines where the bulk of our distance learning courses occur.

33. We collaborate with Outreach faculty and staff to provide in-class instruction, in person, by phone and video, as well as embedded librarian presence in the course shell. We also offer a toll-free reference hotline, live chat reference and email reference. We promote all of those services heavily to outreach students and have created special Web pages both on our site and in the course shell for outreach students doing library research.

34. We provide instruction sessions within the student's classes at the request of the faculty member either at the main campus or via videoconference to our other campuses. (Yes, these are distance students, especially from the library's perspective.) We also do our best to make sure all regular services are as open to them as possible. (For example, they can access our online services seamlessly in

the same way as a non-distance student. We work hard to create services that are inclusive of all our students, not that separate them out unless absolutely necessary.) Databases are all accessible from off-campus, as are interlibrary loan request forms (which we expand to allow distance students to use to request in-library material), we provide multiple ways/media to contact Reference, we have online handouts and tutorials and we keep in mind the distance user group when developing them. We work with faculty to encourage them to integrate information literacy into their curriculum and serve as consultants to help them do so. I'm probably forgetting several things but this is getting long.

35. We have a large number of online databases available to on-campus and distance learning students. We offer virtual reference (via email) and ILL services to off-campus students.

36. We do not currently have any special programs or resources developed for distance learning students.

37. Separate Web page; librarian assigned; e-mail, chat and telephone reference.

38. Noel-Levitz; library surveys; ACRL distance ed training course and standards; solinet training classes.

39. We have a distance learning librarian (position currently vacant) who travels to three other campuses twice per year to do training. Additionally, courses are offered using other technologies.

40. Working with faculty is critical in bringing library resources and services to distance learning students. Well developed research and information assignments are essential. Since DL students do not meet face-to-face, use of services like Elluminate Live! can provide a shared work space experience that deepens understanding of information competencies and library practices.

41. Beside the Ask-a-Librarian service, the answer is none. But, we plan to hire a Distance Learning Librarian for the next academic year and better serving the needs of distance learning students will be the main responsibility of this new hire.

42. We have a blog that anyone can get access to, we have our contact information available and the state provides a listing of people to contact for distance education purposes.

43. Electronic reserves, email and telephone consultations, work with course faculty on library resources for students.

44. Email distance ed instructors once/year to remind them of resources available and how students access them.

45. Ebooks, e journals.

46. We have subscribed to a variety of online reference resources. We have also automated our card catalog so it is available over the Web. Distance learning instructors receive the same library information emails as on-campus instructors. Our Web page has full contact information; so students anywhere can call, fax, email, or snail mail the library for help.

47. We have separate email help screen for distance education students. Any service that is performed within the library is also available for distance students upon request.

48. Fairly extensive library introductory and orientation pages on the Website; full text in catalog; 40% of library's resources are digital (books and journals/databases).

49. Our distant students are primarily located in remote site locations. The librarian visits those sites at the rare invitation of the instructors.

50. We have used the current library literature, practices, and procedures common to the profession that are provided by the Texas Library Association and the Association of College and Research Libraries section of the American Library Association, as well as listservs like Off-Camp to maintain current in the common practices for serving distance learning students. We use current technologies such as a Website with online access to our catalog and databases, podcasting, blogs, virtual chat through Meebo.com for reference service, Blackboard (WebCT) to create instruction and tutorials for all of our students, whether traditional or off-campus.

51. We provide interlibrary loan services and off-campus access to subscription databases and virtual reference sources. We need to do more and concentrate efforts.

52. Resource pages in Blackboard, remote access to research tools, direct mailing to distance learners.

53. Our library uses the Blackboard course software system extensively to work with distance students. As the Education Liaison / Remote Services Librarian I work with faculty to integrate library instructions and librarian help into their course sessions on Blackboard. We have a link to our library homepage listed in every Blackboard course session on campus (blended and distance). In distance courses that require library research we try to set up a librarian-led discussion board forum whenever we can. The one service we provide to distance students beyond what we provide to everyone else is electronic document delivery on journal articles we own only in paper.

54. We have ebooks, e-journals and online ILL and many other instruction and research help that caters to both distance and on-campus students. We provide return postage for books that we loan via ILL. They can call their liaison librarian or use our library reference email option.

55. We have several online research guides and two online tutorials on how to search the catalog. We purchased Camtasia recently and are in the process of creating more tutorials. All online classes have a link to the library's online guide for distance students. The library works with faculty who request a specific research guide for their online class, and we hope to expand this as word spreads of this service. We have a service to mail library materials to distance students and they can do this through a request option in our OPAC.

56. We have only just begun working on a library presence for distance learning students by initiating an embedded librarian program. Reference librarians will participate in individual classes on our courseware in order to provide research/reference knowledge. This will provide personalized service for the students in the electronic environment.

57. We have eight online video tutorials covering document delivery and use of the library's catalog. We make photocopies or send PDF's of articles that we have in

our print journals to distance learners (we do not provide a document delivery service for on-campus patrons). We have been gradually moving most of our journals to online or online-only. We have recently been adding more online reference sources.

58. Online instructions; non-interactive tutorials; blogs; various ways to get help (email, phone, instant message); ILLiad interlibrary loan system; reference assistance.

59. We have extensive online tutorials for research using the school's databases and the Web. We use live chat to answer any questions. Each librarian has a pocket PC to answer questions regardless of the student's location.

60. Toll-free phone calls, email delivery of articles, online forms.

61. DE students may register in Illiad to have materials mailed to them on request, including materials from our own collection.

62. The distance students are supposed to come to school for an orientation on campus. Several classes come to a library workshop about one-third of the way through the quarter. We do get distance learning students using the library. We need to do more to acquaint them with all of the services -- like the access to electronic books, and subscription databases.

63. I have made tutorials using Camtasia. I offer to embed in classes for five days to assist students in finding library resources for their class assignments. We use the campus courier service to deliver library materials to students at our remote sites, and we will mail free of charge to online students living in the United States. We have intergovernmental agreements with five public libraries in the towns where we have a remote instruction center. I visit those public libraries and purchase some academic materials for our students to be placed at those locations. Students can apply for a library card online. When I teach library skills at a remote site location, I make sure they have signed up for their student email account (which is their password for our online databases) and signed up for a library card.

64. Currently, we have a Web page that details options for DL students; however, we are developing an online course using our college's CMS software to be delivered as an option for DL instructors, the same options for their online students as our on-campus students. Also, we hope to make modules for IL and other components available to all students, since we do not get enough time in a 50-minute slot to cover these things in face-to-face instruction.

65. Free book and article delivery to their home or desktop. Email, toll-free phone number and IM. Embedded librarian in Blackboard (online) classes upon request.

66. Web page, chat, personal contacts.

67. We use WebEx teleconferencing to teach info lit courses live. It's very stable, since it was designed for corporate use. Much better than all the other co-browsing software.

68. All electronic resources accessible via proxy service. Citrix solution for accessing campus-licensed software from off-campus will be implemented during Spring 2008.

69. Looking at this now. Electronic Ref librarian is also Blackboard administrator.

70. Chat, email, toll-free number for reference assistance, online tutorials

71. Librarian speaks at DL orientations. Library has Web pages with DL information. There is a link to the Library in Blackboard.

72. We haven't done a lot and could do more.

73. We started virtual ref and the dean killed it. We hired a librarian as a distance ed one, but the dean reappointed her to do circulation. Then she left, another one come and now there is no more talk about it

74. Collaboration with DE faculty and instructional designers to incorporate library into online classrooms. Online tutorials. In-person instruction (for on-campus orientation sessions). Customized course pages. Embedded librarians in online courses.

75. In addition to having most of our databases available to off-campus students (thanks to the proxy server and VPN), we offer a hybrid course equivalent to the on-campus "Library 100/101" non-credit required information literacy curriculum for first-year students.

76. Just beginning an effort to reach distant students by working on getting online tutorials on the Web page and letting instructors know I am available for in-class training in using the library Web resources.

77. Document delivery, phone and email reference, online tutorials, ebooks.

78. All our services and resources are designed for distance learner use. We have an extensive FT online resource collection, offer synchronous training via Wimba virtual classroom, and offer a blog/RSS feed into our CMS for news and research tips.

79. Working with faculty who teach courses; distance education librarian; document delivery services at no charge to the students; chat and email reference; toll-free telephone number; statewide library cooperative borrowing programs

80. CMU's Off Campus Library Services (OCLS) functions as a separate unit dedicated to serving ONLY students who take classes online or at off-campus locations. We offer reference and research assistance via phone, email, Web form and chat, as well as a stand-alone document delivery service for full text articles and books. Library instruction is provided in both face-to-face and online formats for selected classes. The OCLS Website serves as the portal to library resources and services for off-campus students enrolled at 70+ locations in the U.S. and internationally.

81. The library's Coordinator of Distance Education left the library 1 1/2 years ago and we have not implemented any new programs for distance students besides a Web page outlining services.

82. Collaboration with faculty in resource selection and marketing.

83. Last year we created and published a CD guide to library and research services for distance ed students, distributed by the faculties in enrolment packs. (Many of our distance ed students are in remote and regional areas without broadband services; the CD was intended to give them quick, and cheap, access to large docs, applications and CBT available. We have a part-time position of Off Campus Library Liaison who acts a coordination point for off-campus and microcampus students, travels to the microcampuses, keeps microcampus staff informed of developments, and gives face-to-face training as well as educating campus library staff on the specific needs of off-campus students.

84. Appointing a Distance Learning librarian whose primary responsibility is assisting distance learners is the major step my library has taken. Very helpful is being able to call on our almost 100 databases of journal articles and electronic rcsources (including many full text articles and electronic books). However, my most valuable practice is making myself available to students as much as possible. I will take telephone calls anytime I'm available, and respond to emails during all working hours and on my own time.

1. Brochures enclosed in every distance student's package; 2. Links to the library's distance services on every WebCT page; 3. A specialized "Doing Research at a Distance" guide; 4. Facebook profile & group; 5. Extended loan lengths for students at a distance; 6. Chat reverence via QuestionPoint and Meebo; 7. Website; 8. Work with instructional designers to interstate library resources in an accessible way.

85. We have put links to the library on all online courses. We offer e-mail reference service on our Web page. We are planning to become "embedded" librarians in several courses.

86. Nothing additional to what is above. I have tried to work with the Dist. Ed dept but they are not receptive. There is no way to work with c-College to provide modules on learning, and contacts to the adjunct faculty usually are ignored. The best response is from those faculty who offer classes via satellite, since we can do some standard one-shot sessions that way. Internet online-only classes do not use our services that way.

Chapter Three: Relating to Distance Learning Instructors

Over a third of our sample considered distance learning instructors less likely than traditional course instructors to approach the library when they need help. Just 6% of the sample reported that distance learning instructors were more likely to seek help from the library. The majority, almost 59%, reported that they were just as likely as traditional course instructors to approach the library when in need of help. U.S. respondents were 40% more likely than non-U.S. survey participants to say that distance learning instructors were less likely than traditional instructors to seek help from the library. Non-U.S. libraries, in fact, reported a rate 4 times higher than U.S. libraries when indicating that distance learning instructors were more likely to seek out help from the library, compared to traditional course instructors.

Over 44% of community colleges and half of the four-year degree granting colleges reported distance learning instructors were less likely than traditional course instructors to seek help from them. Almost 30% of MA or PhD-granting colleges and nearly 24% of research universities reported the same. No community college or four-year degree-granting college reported that their distance learning instructors were more likely than traditional course instructors to seek help from the library. However, almost 12% of MA or PhD-granting colleges and 10% of research universities reported that their distance learning instructors were more likely than traditional course instructors to seek them out for help.

48% of private colleges believe their distance learning instructors were less likely than traditional course instructors to approach the library when they need help, while 44% believed that they were as likely to seek help. For public colleges, however, 64% reported that distance learning instructors were just as likely as traditional course instructors to seek help from them, and only 30.56% thought they were less likely to approach the library for help.

Distance learning instructors appeared less ikely to approach the library at larger institutions. Almost 42% of institutions with more than 12,000 FTE students, and a third of the institutions with fewer than 2,500 FTE students, were less likely than traditional students to approach the library for help. However, 28%, of students at institutions with between 6,001 and 12,000 FTE students are less likely than traditional students to seek help.

When asked about any special efforts that the library has made to reach out to distance learning instructors, survey participants reported that maintaining some kind of contact with students and sending reminders of the resources offered by the library were the most consistent answers.

We asked the sample to explain how the library helps distance learners to access online course notes, course-specific Websites, online course bibliographies, or any other information posted online by the instructor or Website itself. The most common answer given was through software course management systems, most often Blackboard and WebCT. E-reserves through these applications was the most frequently given answer to the response, though many also responded that help was available through online help pages, chat, email and phone, either for the student wishing to access resources or for instructors wishing to use them. Some respondents offered print instructions, courses and web seminars, and in-person presentations as well. Still others did little to nothing in this regard, because such Web pages are managed by the instructor directly or by another entity, such as the e-college.

Table 3.1:   Relationship Between the Library and Distance Learning Instructors vs. Instructors of Traditional Courses

	Are less likely to approach the library when they need help	Are more likely to approach the library when they need help	Are about as likely as instructors of traditional courses to approach the library when they need help
Entire Sample	35.05%	6.19%	58.76%

Table 3.2:   Relationship Between the Library and Distance Learning Instructors vs. Instructors of Traditional Courses, Broken Out by U.S. and Non-U.S. Libraries

U.S. and Non-U.S. Libraries	Are less likely to approach the library when they need help	Are more likely to approach the library when they need help	Are about as likely as instructors of traditional courses to approach the library when they need help
U.S.	37.18%	3.85%	58.97%
Non-U.S.	26.32%	15.79%	57.89%

Table 3.3:   Relationship Between the Library and Distance Learning Instructors vs. Instructors of Traditional Courses, Broken Out by Carnegie Class

Carnegie Class	Are less likely to approach the library when they need help	Are more likely to approach the library when they need help	Are about as likely as instructors of traditional courses to approach the library when they need help
Community College	44.12%	0.00%	55.88%
4-Year Degree Granting College	50.00%	0.00%	50.00%
MA or PhD Granting College	29.41%	11.76%	58.82%
Research University	23.81%	9.52%	66.67%

Table 3.4: Relationship Between the Library and Distance Learning Instructors vs. Instructors of Traditional Courses, Broken Out by Public or Private Status

Public or Private Status	Are less likely to approach the library when they need help	Are more likely to approach the library when they need help	Are about as likely as instructors of traditional courses to approach the library when they need help
Public College	30.56%	5.56%	63.89%
Private College	48.00%	8.00%	44.00%

Table 3.5: Relationship Between the Library and Distance Learning Instructors vs. Instructors of Traditional Courses, Broken Out by Number of FTE Students at the Institution

Number of FTE Students at the Institution	Are less likely to approach the library when they need help	Are more likely to approach the library when they need help	Are about as likely as instructors of traditional courses to approach the library when they need help
>12,000	41.67%	4.17%	54.17%
6,001-12,000	28.00%	4.00%	68.00%
2,500-6,000	37.50%	8.33%	54.17%
<2500	33.33%	8.33%	58.33%

Table 3.6: Relationship Between the Library and Distance Learning Instructors vs. Instructors of Traditional Courses, Broken Out by Number of FTE Distance Learners

Number of FTE Distance Learners	Are less likely to approach the library when they need help	Are more likely to approach the library when they need help	Are about as likely as instructors of traditional courses to approach the library when they need help
>2,000	50.00%	0.00%	50.00%
1,000-2,000	36.84%	5.26%	57.89%
250-999	20.00%	10.00%	70.00%
<250	40.00%	10.00%	50.00%

Survey of Library Services for Distance Learning Programs

Table 3.7: Relationship Between the Library and Distance Learning Instructors vs. Instructors of Traditional Courses, Broken Out by Percentage of Distance Learners Living More than 50 Miles from Campus

Percentage of Distance Learners Living More than 50 Miles from Campus	Are less likely to approach the library when they need help	Are more likely to approach the library when they need help	Are about as likely as instructors of traditional courses to approach the library when they need help
80-100%	26.09%	8.70%	65.22%
51-79%	17.65%	11.76%	70.59%
25-50%	50.00%	4.55%	45.45%
1-24%	30.00%	0.00%	70.00%

Answers to the prompt, "Has the library made any special efforts to reach out to instructors of distance learning courses? If so, explain what you did and what were the results."

1. Make faculty aware of online library resources and services.
2. Many of our full-time faculty teach "distance" courses. The main problem is getting to adjuncts. Some programs do a good job of advertising library services that support faculty and their students.
3. A librarian sits as a member of the Online Program Coordinators group. This group provides support to online faculty and students. In a roundabout way, a dialogue exists between the library and distance students/faculty.
4. All of the online courses are designed by one course designer. The library has bimonthly meetings with this designer. The designer has been very good about adding guides and Weblinks to all of the ANGEL courses for online students.
5. It's difficult to know who is teaching what, especially with online programs that contract distant adjunct instructors.
6. We have offered information literacy workshops for faculty. 60% of the faculty attended a four-session workshop over a three-year period. Many of these faculty teach distance courses.
7. Yes, partnering with instructional designers to ensure that every distance instructor knows about the library and feels free to involve the Distance Education Librarian in course development, etc.
8. Inductions and awareness sessions for lecturers.
9. We do have meetings with the distance education program directors. Emails are sent semesterly to distance instructors providing information about library services.
10. We contact every distance learning instructor and let them know what library services are available to them and their students.
11. Email.
12. We have tried to get links to library resources into courseware. After years, there now appears to be some interest, and we may be implementing library info in the next few months.
13. I will be emailing the instructors next week to offer my assistance in this area.

14. Visits to department meetings and emails to the instructors of distance courses listserv. Have had limited but positive responses.
15. Yes, we have offered to become involved in their Blackboard courses and offer to help find full text articles when the course is being developed.
16. Work through Distance Ed dept and send out special handbook for instructors about library services; include them in faculty mail-outs. This has resulted in more questions from them and more use from their students.
17. I send letters out to all off-campus faculty each year, outlining services to distance students.
18. No special efforts beyond what we do to connect with all instructors.
19. Yes, we approach the instructors of distance learning courses to remind them of the importance of coordinating with the library. Most of the time this has been successful.
20. Yes; librarians with subject/dept liaison assignments contact faculty and specifically reach out to instructors of distance ed classes to offer library support. We have plans for a couple of librarians to visit our university's three regional campuses (we have also 16 distance ed sites distributed throughout the state). As a land grant institution, we have a strong Extension program, and librarians are in communication with extension faculty to promote research support.
21. Not to our knowledge.
22. Liaison assignments with colleges and units; attendance and participation in college and departmental meetings; faculty workshops.
23. The library participated in a technology-enhances learning and distance learning forum recently, where we presented on DL services.
24. Participate in in-service or orientation of instructors who teach distance classes, maintain liaisons to distance programs.
25. Requesting bibliographies.
26. The librarian liaison to those departments that teach distance learning courses regularly prepares Web pages and video tutorials, which have received positive feedback from students.
27. Contacted by phone and email.
28. We contact them directly every semester and through their local coordinators. It has been a positive result.
29. Again, it depends on your definition of "distance learning" but we contact all faculty, including the adjuncts on a regular basis to remind them of our instructional and information literacy services and on an irregular basis as other needs, issues, or situations come up.
30. Not recently; prior response was minimal.
31. Technical Assistance with Podcasting.
32. Direct and mass emailings.
33. Yes. Met with instructors in the other campuses, offering "train the trainer" courses.
34. Absolutely! Without cooperation and support from DL faculty, the students would be less likely to use the library.
35. No special efforts; outreach is to all faculty, traditional and online.
36. No, not at this time.

37. Yes. Offer resource pages, consultations, bibliographic assistance, online resources. Positively received; some used.
38. All are treated equally.
39. No. As indicated above, the library's outreach is the same for instructors both on and off campus.
40. We contact the professors each semester through their blackboard course shell. Some professors jumped at the chance for help and others ignored it.
41. Emailed all DE instructors suggesting linking to the library on Blackboard sites. Do not know the results.
42. Yes, regular emails, calls.
43. Yes. We have a designated librarian that serves on the campus's Distance Learning Committee as a liaison to the Distance Learning instructors. Through this committee, the librarian is able to share library resources and services with the instructors, as well as, determine their needs.
44. Not yet.
45. During orientation we covered library services and resources.
46. Our university made a commitment to have only full time on-campus faculty teach online courses. We have an occasional adjunct but they are usually doctoral students with whom I am acquainted.
47. Yes, the instructors are advised of the library services via the DL office. Instructors have requested that a librarian be part of their webct course. A librarian can be signed up as a TA such that library-related questions can be answered in a timely manner. This program is very successful when it is used.
48. We have done targeted outreach to faculty teaching courses that might have a research component, and thus a need for library resources.
49. Our embedded librarian program for distance learners has only just begun and so rolling out the program as a pilot.
50. I sent email messages outlining library services. I also met with our instructors who teach at off-campus sites to tell them about library services and demo some simple searches. I think the instructors inform the students, but I don't think it has increased the use of the distance learning librarian's direct services.
51. We attend the orientations, and encourage the students to use the library. I encourage instructors to bring their class for a library workshop after they have assigned a research project.
52. Whenever I do a presentation to the faculty I always mention that I can collaborate with them for distance class library assignment. I have been doing this for about two years and it takes time. Some of it is word of mouth, a faculty member is pleased with the results and tells their peers. I just designed a small marketing brochure of library services for distance students and it is being given out to all faculty also at semester start-up. I am placing my tutorials in the section of Blackboard where faculty share things, so anyone can use the tutorials in their class. I teach a session or two on new library and Internet resources or copyright each summer at the week-long camp for online instructors.
53. I created an online library module that could be imported into Blackboard. It was offered to distance and campus instructors for their online courses. It was implemented in some, but no real way of knowing its use.

54. Not yet, other than positing a link on our Website. We have plans in the future to market our services once the online class is developed.
55. Email them each semester with list of library services for distance ed. Create a newsletter each semester targeted at DE students and faculty.
56. Yes, attend orientation sessions; mentor new DE faculty
57. Primarily through training in use of Desire2Learn CMS software and in creating proxied links to full text content.
58. Electronic Ref Librarian teaching Blackboard classes & putting library resources into DL courses
59. Yes, several presentations, email. We've had little interest from faculty.
60. Sent email and speak about it whenever/wherever possible, but not much interest.
61. Sporadic, chaotic, nonexistent efforts.
62. Yes. Email contact. Member of support team (with instructional designers) for faculty converting courses to online. Results are mixed. Some faculty do not include library resources to a great extent beyond e-reserve. Some faculty have incorporated the library in a number of ways.
63. The School of Continuing Studies actually has hired a librarian specifically to interact with the distance ed students and faculty. I contact every faculty member on the course schedule and offer whatever help I can, in a personalized way, for their class and students. Often, I will drive to an off-campus site to do "one-shot" courses tailored to specific assignments.
64. All of our instructors are at a distance. We are trying various communication methods to reach them. It is too soon for results.
65. We offer workshops for faculty, travel to our state-wide office locations for consultations, man tables at the college's faculty events, etc.
66. Receive list of faculty each term who are teaching distance education classes, send messages to faculty, some respond.
67. CMU's Off Campus Library Services program markets its services to off-campus students and faculty through faculty newsletters, instruction sessions, and participation in collaborative projects and training.
68. All our distance instructors are teaching on campus courses as well.
69. No organized attempt so far...
70. Contact the tutors via email to let them know about our services, present at tutor workshops, enclose copies of faculty and student distance service brochures upon employment, etc.
71. We have not done anything specific, but plan to send letters to online instructors.
72. Yes. I have tried to e-mail them, send fliers, brochures etc. Only the occasional instructor has responded, usually just to get set up as a library user, and that's the last we hear from them.

Answers to the prompt, "Explain how the library helps distance learning students to access online course notes, course-specific Websites, online course bibliographies and other information posted online by the instructor or by the library itself."

Survey of Library Services for Distance Learning Programs

1. The students have access to online course content through Blackboard. I believe that every Blackboard course that students take has a link to the library Web page or specific library Web pages. I am not aware of any online course that has links to specific bibliographies, but there may be some.
2. Direct work with faculty. Build links into courses.
3. Blackboard is the name of the game. E-reserves are now available through BB's "content collection" tools, so many things are incorporated into Blackboard. Some of us are embedded in courses, though we haven't done too much of this. We have provided specialized PowerPoints, Websites, PDF files for some classes.
    Example: I actively assisted a distance learning class offered in Research Methods in Music and Music Ed by preparing handouts uploaded into Bb. I also held an Elluminate session for the class and used email and phone to talk to some class members.
4. Librarians are available via phone and email to point students to relevant information. Library Web Team works to ensure the library Website is intuitively constructed so students may quickly find relevant information.
5. The largest online program we have has a two-week long on-site residency. During this residency, the students are shown how to access these research aids.
6. The library has a presence in Blackboard, the course management software.
7. Instructors handle their own Blackboard sites and information. The library has a Blackboard site, but it is undergoing renovation and is not currently available.
8. E-Reserves is very heavily used for distance learning students. All graduate courses have a WebCT component. Develops special library Websites for online courses; maintains an "Ask a Librarian" thread in WebCT.
9. Via Intruction sheets, phone or email support, Web pages.
10. Web pages. Some contact to the students through the instructors. Embedding in WebCT courses.
11. All course material is available via The Learning Manager and library materials are accessed via the library Website.
12. Created how-to pages.
13. The library has a tab in Blackboard, our college's course management system. The faculty handle all of the postings for their course materials themselves.
14. The only thing that we would do in this respect would be to provide copyright cleared material in the appropriate VLE.
15. E-learning.
16. We have no specific procedure for this.
17. Assistance depends on the needs of the student.
18. The College uses BlackBoard and a Library Help section has been put into the template of each course. This includes a link to the library and some instruction. In courses in which the DL has been invited to participate, the course will also have online research guides that are specifically developed for the course and directions for requesting books from the library.
19. Library has no involvement with online information posted by instructors. Library's online information is on Website.
20. We use Blackboard, and I work with faculty to develop RefShare reading lists that work through our Resolver to the full text of resources.

21. Instructors post to Blackboard, so students access material through that portal. Students have remote access through the library Website to subject guides and selected Weblinks, as well as to tutoring reviews and materials.

22. Our distance learning students have a staff person (not library staff) dedicated to providing technical support to them.

23. We use several tools, some redundant, including: links from the BlackBoard course management system (the central BB template links to the library, and individual instructors often include library links; online course reserves; LibGuides Web pages created by librarian for specific courses and disciplines to promote databases, e-journals, interlibrary loan, and options for research consultation.

24. These services are provided through the university's student portal.

25. Students have access to Blackboard for course materials and a library e-reserve system.

26. The library provides assistance for electronic reserves services, but not for materials posted on course-management systems.

27. E-reserves are posted on BlackBoard by the library; other course information is posted on BlackBoard by the instructor. The library conducts on-site workshops for research classes and advertises its email address and phone number widely.

28. Promoted by the instructor.

29. Mainly we do this through subject-specific resources guides posted to our Website in PDF form, for example .http://rattler.tamucc.edu/elecres/resourceguides/nursing/NursingRG_1207.pdf.

30. We provide online instruction.

31. We explain to them the basics of how to connect to their online classrooms and, if they have problems beyond that, refer them to the departments on campus who have the responsibility and access to help them with these things.

32. We respond to e-mail requests for aid in accessing the mentioned services.

33. The significant majority of online databases are available remotely.

34. All courses are through Blackboard; electronic reserves included.

35. Provide virtual reserve material.

36. Hour and a half online course.

37. Electronic reserve is the primary tool for this. The University also uses Blackboard, with library links.

38. We help students who ask for help. And when we anticipate the kinds of assistance students may ask about, we create FAQs, guides, and other online services.

39. We're planning to implement e-reserves in 2008-2009.

40. No special effort has been made in this area but we have a very small distance education clientele.

41. Help guides online, messages for instructors to use inside their online courses.

42. We have class pages specific to the resources used by a class OR even to a specific class research assignment; the class pages list best online library databases to use.

43. This access is the responsibility of the instructor.

44. We like to think that our library's Website is intuitive, and that help (clearly marked "help") would be easy to locate, whether distance education or traditional student.

45. Most instructors use Blackboard site for most materials. The library provides online course reserves as needed. Probably most DE instructors are providing their materials on their Website.

46. The DL Librarian sends broadcast emails to all students about online access to library resources and services. The library also has a library link within WebCT that all students can access from the front page and that DL instructors can integrate into their WebCT courses.

47. We provide access through a proxy server for subscription resources and have just posted our first course-specific online bibliography.

48. Through faculty awareness and contacts.

49. Through Blackboard course software.

50. Professors must work with his or her subject liaison librarian to get all the library-related resources that is needed for a class.

51. We have no access to the online course shell. Due to FERPA, we were recently told that no one except those enrolled in a course and the instructor for that course can be allowed to access the online course. This limits how available and connected we can be with students. Instructors are required to link to the library's general guide to services for distance learners. We are trying to offer chat reference, but our IT department blocks all chat because they believe it is a security threat. We are working on a proposal that we hope will convince them otherwise. We do not have electronic reserves, but we have a large ebook collection and many research databases.

52. The library manages our WebCT and Blackboard servers, and assists the instructors with planning their online courses if the instructors so choose. (We have an instructional developer on staff.) We have a link for online courses on the library's home page. If students need help specifically with the online course pages, we have an email help ticket service and an instant messaging help service on the log-in page for the online courses. The library also has a separate instant messaging service open to students, faculty, staff, and the public, as well as email reference.

53. We instruct them on how to find such things as best we can. If we can't help them (particularly with information posted by instructors), we may refer them back to the instructor or to a Distance Learning advisor.

54. We assist distance learners, or e-learners, with their email, connecting to our CMS, and library usage. We have an extensive eReserves area on the Website.

55. Print instructions, PowerPoint demos, online chat, catalogs, Websites.

56. Most of this is handled by individual instructors on Blackboard, without significant library involvement.

57. We use WebCT. Students can access their grades, course notes, streaming video (where applicable), etc.

58. At this time we are not involved in any e-reserves or course-specific Websites for the students. We facilitate their access to our electronic resources through a proxy server which authenticates them by their email user ID and password.

59. An electronic reserve system is available for instructors to place articles online.

60. We try to assist students in person or on the phone with what we can; our DL staff is excellent for helping students as well, in person or via phone.

61. most course info is in blackboard course management system. I am embedded in some blackboard courses and create a library section where I add tutorials, links and explanations of how to access the library from home, how to search for journals articles and other research, streaming tutorials, links to course reserve readings, citation styles, etc.

62. Little is done here.

63. Mainly by virtual reference.

64. E-Reserves and Media Streaming authenticate through campus directory, same as proxied services and Desire2Learn course management system.

65. Develop specific links to specific articles/books as well as single sign-on for Blackboard/Library databases.

66. We provide links to our tutorials and we offer one-on-one assistance. We work with professors to ensure that materials are available through e-reserves or with permanent links embedded in CMS.

67. Give out my email address. Have tutorials about how to access databases, catalog, etc.

68. We have an outreach librarian who goes to the various locations to provide such an orientation at the beginning of the year and at other times during the year.

69. Nothing. Librarians claim being stretched thin. Big turnover does not help concentrating on the issue.

70. We offer e-reserve. We have a link on all D2L courses to the library.

71. We point students (and actively teach them about) our Research Guides by Subject/Major, and these are heavily used.

72. No specific help unless they call in. We have provided an email for help but it has not been used at all.

73. Direct links to the library from our course management system and from the student's start page. Our reference service does a lot of this and we do live lectures at the FTF get-togethers of our PhD students.

74. We work with course developers to choose appropriate resources and how to effectively embed them into the content as well as infuse the content with info skills activities where appropriate.

75. Instructor handles all of this in Blackboard; library provides electronic reserve lists for classes.

76. CMU's Off Campus Library Services facilitates access to course materials through Blackboard by handling copyright clearance, scanning, and Interlibrary Loan requests for off-campus faculty. The Course Pack Coordinator posts course materials on behalf of faculty as requested. Materials not posted through Blackboard are requested and delivered via the OCLS Document Delivery service.

77. The library does not play a role in this area. Campus IT maintains the Blackboard site and provides all assistance. The library hosts online course reserves, but I don't think distance instructors use this service extensively. The library provides

support/help to students who are trying to log in to use the library's resources when off-campus.

78. Much of this occurs via WebCT.

79. We try to make our Website, and orientation material, neutral to the nature of the study i.e., on-campus, remote, flexible learning and microcampus students have equitable access to everything we provide.

80. Our library doesn't usually get involved in this process unless the instructor asks us. Our course management software (Blackboard) is handled by our IT dept., so they deal with most of these issues. However, I have in the past set up password-protected Web pages to expedite distance students' access to articles we don't own in electronic form.

81. We have a specialized "Research at a Distance" guide, discipline specific research guides, within courses, there are links to relevant library guides, etc.

82. We don't do anything like this.

83. Nothing. All this is handled via e-college.

Chapter Four: Orientation

Over a third of the sample had an equivalent to the traditional orientation program for new distance learners. Over 40% of U.S. libraries and 16% of non-U.S. libraries had an orientation program for distance learners. Community colleges, at 44%, were most likely to have such an orientation program. Thirty-seven percent of MA or PhD-granting, 29% of four-year colleges and 23% of research universities offered orientation sessions for distance learners. More than 32% of public colleges and 44% of private colleges had student orientation for distance learners.

There was no direct relationship between the availability of such an orientation program for new distance learners and the number of FTE students at the institution. In fact, while the highest percentage, 40%, was reported by institutions with between 6,001 and 12,000 FTE students, the lowest percentage, just under 32%, was reported by institutions with over 12,000 FTE students. A more discernable pattern emerged as the sample was broken out by number of FTE distance learners, however. Orientation programs were most prevalent among institutions with fewer than 250 FTE distance learners; over 52% had a program. By comparison, almost 28% of institutions with over 2,000 FTE distance learners had an orientation program for distance learners. There was no clear relationship between proportions of the distance learning students living more than 50 miles away and the availability of an orientation program for new distance learners.

Just under half of the libraries play a role in the orientation of distance learners. Non-U.S. libraries were over 50% more likely to play a role in distance learning student orientation. While between 50 and 54% of four-year degree-granting collages, MA or PhD-granting colleges, and research universities reported that their libraries played a role in distance learner orientation, just 39% of community colleges reported the same. There was no significant difference between data gathered from public and private colleges regarding the library's role in the orientation of distance learners, though private college libraries were just slightly more likely to be involved than public college libraries.

The lowest percentage of colleges with libraries involved in distance learner orientation, 45.8%, was reported by colleges with over 12,000 FTE students. However, 52% of colleges with between 6,001 and 12,000 students reported the same, as did 48% of students with between 2,500 and 6,000 students, and 50% of colleges with fewer than 2,500 students. Fully two out of three colleges with more than 2,000 FTE distance learners, the highest reported incidence, had libraries involved in the orientation programs of distance learners. By comparison, just 42% of colleges with between 1,000 and 2,000 FTE distance learners, 45% of colleges with between 250 and 999 FTE distance learners, and 52% of colleges with fewer than 250 FTE distance learners reported the same. The library's involvement with distance learner orientation generally increased when the proportion of distance learners living more than 50 miles away from campus was over 50% of their distance learning student population.

Survey of Library Services for Distance Learning Programs

Table 4.1: Percentage of Libraries with an Equivalent of the Traditional Orientation Program for New Distance Learners

	Yes	No
Entire Sample	35.42%	64.58%

Table 4.2: Percentage of Libraries with an Equivalent of the Traditional Orientation Program for New Distance Learners, Broken Out by U.S. and Non-U.S. Libraries

U.S. and Non-U.S. Libraries	Yes	No
U.S.	40.26%	59.74%
Non-U.S.	15.79%	84.21%

Table 4.3: Percentage of Libraries with an Equivalent of the Traditional Orientation Program for New Distance Learners, Broken Out by Carnegie Class

Carnegie Class	Yes	No
Community College	43.75%	56.25%
4-Year Degree Granting College	28.57%	71.43%
MA or PhD Granting College	37.14%	62.86%
Research University	22.73%	77.27%

Table 4.4: Percentage of Libraries with an Equivalent of the Traditional Orientation Program for New Distance Learners, Broken Out by Public or Private Status

Public or Private Status	Yes	No
Public College	32.39%	67.61%
Private College	44.00%	56.00%

Table 4.5: Percentage of Libraries with an Equivalent of the Traditional Orientation Program for New Distance Learners, Broken Out by Number of FTE Students at the Institution

Number of FTE Students at the Institution	Yes	No
>12,000	31.82%	68.18%
6,001-12,000	40.00%	60.00%
2,500-6,000	36.00%	64.00%
<2,500	33.33%	66.67%

Table 4.6: Percentage of Libraries with an Equivalent of the Traditional Orientation Program for New Distance Learners, Broken Out by Number of FTE Distance Learners

Number of FTE Distance Learners	Yes	No
>2,000	27.78%	72.22%
1,000-2,000	36.84%	63.16%
250-999	30.00%	70.00%
<250	52.38%	47.62%

Table 4.7: Percentage of Libraries with an Equivalent of the Traditional Orientation Program for New Distance Learners, Broken Out by Percentage of Distance Learners Living More than 50 Miles from Campus

Percentage of Distance Learners Living More than 50 Miles from Campus	Yes	No
80-100%	39.13%	60.87%
51-79%	41.18%	58.82%
25-50%	26.09%	73.91%
1-24%	42.11%	57.89%

Table 4.8: Percentage of Libraries that Play a Role in the Orientation of Distance Learners

	Yes	No
Entire Sample	48.98%	51.02%

Table 4.9: Percentage of Libraries that Play a Role in the Orientation of Distance Learners, Broken Out by U.S. and Non-U.S. Libraries

U.S. and Non-U.S. Libraries	Yes	No
U.S.	44.30%	55.70%
Non-U.S.	68.42%	31.58%

Table 4.10: Percentage of Libraries that Play a Role in the Orientation of Distance Learners, Broken Out by Carnegie Class

Carnegie Class	Yes	No
Community College	39.39%	60.61%
4-Year Degree Granting College	50.00%	50.00%
MA or PhD Granting College	54.29%	45.71%
Research University	54.55%	45.45%

Table 4.11: Percentage of Libraries that Play a Role in the Orientation of Distance Learners, Broken Out by Public or Private Status

Public or Private Status	Yes	No
Public College	48.61%	51.39%
Private College	50.00%	50.00%

Table 4.12: Percentage of Libraries that Play a Role in the Orientation of Distance Learners, Broken Out by Number of FTE Students at the Institution

Number of FTE Students at the Institution	Yes	No
>12,000	45.83%	54.17%
6,001-12,000	52.00%	48.00%
2,500-6,000	48.00%	52.00%
<2500	50.00%	50.00%

Table 4.13: Percentage of Libraries that Play a Role in the Orientation of Distance Learners, Broken Out by Number of FTE Distance Learners

Number of FTE Distance Learners	Yes	No
>2,000	66.67%	33.33%
1,000-2,000	42.11%	57.89%
250-999	45.00%	55.00%
<250	52.38%	47.62%

Table 4.14: Percentage of Libraries that Play a Role in the Orientation of Distance Learners, Broken Out by Percentage of Distance Learners Living More than 50 Miles from Campus

Percentage of Distance Learners Living More than 50 Miles from Campus	Yes	No
80-100%	65.22%	34.78%
51-79%	82.35%	17.65%
25-50%	39.13%	60.87%
1-24%	30.00%	70.00%

Chapter Five: Arranging Physical Library Facilities for Distance Learners

Just over half of the sample, 53%, maintained agreements with other libraries to offer services to the college's distance learners. While just 48% of U.S. libraries had these agreements, almost 74% of non-U.S.libraries did. A similarly high percentage of four-year degree-granting colleges, 75%, had agreements with other libraries to offer library services to the college's distance learners. Just under 60% of research universities did, as did 48.5% of both community colleges and MA or PhD-granting colleges. Public colleges were nearly twice as likely as private colleges to have such agreements with other libraries, with 61% of public colleges and 31% of private colleges reporting such.

There was no clear linear relationship between the college's number of FTE students and the college's maintenance of agreements with other libraries to offer library service to the college's distance learners. While 64% of colleges with between 6,001 and 12,000 FTE students had such agreements, the lowest percentage, 44%, was reported by the tier just below that, by colleges with between 2,500 and 6,000 FTE students. Just over 54% of colleges with over 12,000 FTE students and 50% of colleges with under 2,500 FTE students reported the same.

Similarly, there was no linear relationship between number of FTE distance learners and agreements with other libraries to offer services to the college's distance learners. While 60% of colleges with between 250 and 999 FTE distance learners had agreements with other libraries to offer services to their distance learners, the lowest percentage, 47%, was reported by the colleges with between 1,000 and 2,000 FTE distance learners. Over 55% of colleges with over 2,000 FTE distance learners and 52% of colleges with fewer than 250 FTE distance learners reported the same. Almost 70% of colleges with over 80% of their distance learners living more than 50 miles away maintained agreements with other libraries to offer library services to the college's distance learners. Just 47% of colleges with between 51 and 79% of their distance learners living more than 50 miles away reported the same.

Almost 64% of the sample provided library access or services to students enrolled in other colleges' distance learning programs. While almost 62% of U.S. libraries reported doing so, almost 74% of non-U.S. libraries in the sample did. Almost 68% of MA and PhD-granting colleges and 67% of community colleges offered library access or services to other colleges' distance learners, compared to 62.5% of four-year degree granting colleges and just 54.6% of research universities. Public colleges led the way, with over 66% of public colleges offering such access or services, compared with almost 58% of private colleges.

The percentages reporting to provide library access or services were uniform for schools of all FTE enrollment sizes, except for colleges with between 2,500 and 6,000 FTE students. While all other sized colleges reported between 67% and 68%, just 54% of colleges with between 2,500 and 6,000 FTE students offered library access or services to the distance learning students of any other colleges.

Survey of Library Services for Distance Learning Programs

Colleges with a smaller number of students enrolled in distance learning tended to be more likely to have reciprocal agreements to provide library services to the distance learning students of other colleges. Over 90% of colleges with fewer than 250 FTE distance learners offered their library access or services to students enrolled in other colleges' distance learning programs, but just 47% of colleges with between 250 and 999 FTE distance learners reported the same, as did 63% of colleges with between 1,000 and 2,000 FTE distance learners and over 55% of colleges with over 2,000 FTE distance learners.

Table 5.1:   Percentage of Libraries that Maintain Agreements with Other Libraries to Offer Library Services to Any of the College's Distance Learners

	Yes	No
Entire Sample	53.06%	46.94%

Table 5.2:   Percentage of Libraries that Maintain Agreements with Other Libraries to Offer Library Services to Any of the College's Distance Learners, Broken Out by U.S. and Non-U.S. Libraries

U.S. and Non-U.S. Libraries	Yes	No
U.S.	48.10%	51.90%
Non-U.S.	73.68%	26.32%

Table 5.3:   Percentage of Libraries that Maintain Agreements with Other Libraries to Offer Library Services to Any of the College's Distance Learners, Broken Out by Carnegie Class

Carnegie Class	Yes	No
Community College	48.48%	51.52%
4-Year Degree Granting College	75.00%	25.00%
MA or PhD Granting College	48.57%	51.43%
Research University	59.09%	40.91%

Table 5.4:   Percentage of Libraries that Maintain Agreements with Other Libraries to Offer Library Services to Any of the College's Distance Learners, Broken Out by Public or Private Status

Public or Private Status	Yes	No
Public College	61.11%	38.89%
Private College	30.77%	69.23%

Table 5.5: **Percentage of Libraries that Maintain Agreements with Other Libraries to Offer Library Services to Any of the College's Distance Learners, Broken Out by Number of FTE Students at the Institution**

Number of FTE Students at the Institution	Yes	No
>12,000	54.17%	45.83%
6,001-12,000	64.00%	36.00%
2,500-6,000	44.00%	56.00%
<2,500	50.00%	50.00%

Table 5.6: **Percentage of Libraries that Maintain Agreements with Other Libraries to Offer Library Services to Any of the College's Distance Learners, Broken Out by Number of FTE Distance Learners**

Number of FTE Distance Learners	Yes	No
>2,000	55.56%	44.44%
1,000-2,000	47.37%	52.63%
250-999	60.00%	40.00%
<250	52.38%	47.62%

Table 5.7: **Percentage of Libraries that Maintain Agreements with Other Libraries to Offer Library Services to Any of the College's Distance Learners, Broken Out by Percentage of Distance Learners Living More than 50 Miles from Campus**

Percentage of Distance Learners Living More than 50 Miles from Campus	Yes	No
80-100%	69.57%	30.43%
51-79%	47.06%	52.94%
25-50%	52.17%	47.83%
1-24%	50.00%	50.00%

Table 5.8: **Percentage of Libraries that Provide Library Access or Services to Students Enrolled in Other Colleges' Distance Learning Programs**

	Yes	No
Entire Sample	63.92%	36.08%

petaSurvey of Library Services for Distance Learning Programs

Table 5.9:   Percentage of Libraries that Provide Library Access or
Services to Students Enrolled in Other Colleges' Distance Learning Programs,
Broken Out by U.S. and Non-U.S. Libraries

U.S. and Non-U.S. Libraries	Yes	No
U.S.	61.54%	38.46%
Non-U.S.	73.68%	26.32%

Table 5.10:   Percentage of Libraries that Provide Library Access or
Services to Students Enrolled in Other Colleges' Distance Learning Programs,
Broken Out by Carnegie Class

Carnegie Class	Yes	No
Community College	66.67%	33.33%
4-Year Degree Granting College	62.50%	37.50%
MA or PhD Granting College	67.65%	32.35%
Research University	54.55%	45.45%

Table 5.11:   Percentage of Libraries that Provide Library Access or
Services to Students Enrolled in Other Colleges' Distance Learning Programs,
Broken Out by Public or Private Status

Public or Private Status	Yes	No
Public College	66.20%	33.80%
Private College	57.69%	42.31%

Table 5.12:   Percentage of Libraries that Provide Library Access or
Services to Students Enrolled in Other Colleges' Distance Learning Programs,
Broken Out by Number of FTE Students at the Institution

Number of FTE Students at the Institution	Yes	No
>12,000	66.67%	33.33%
6,001-12,000	68.00%	32.00%
2,500-6,000	54.17%	45.83%
<2,500	66.67%	33.33%

Table 5.13:   Percentage of Libraries that Provide Library Access or
Services to Students Enrolled in Other Colleges' Distance Learning Programs,
Broken Out by Number of FTE Distance Learners

Number of FTE Distance Learners	Yes	No
>2,000	55.56%	44.44%
1,000-2,000	63.16%	36.84%
250-999	47.37%	52.63%
<250	90.48%	9.52%

Table 5.14: Percentage of Libraries that Provide Library Access or Services to Students Enrolled in Other Colleges' Distance Learning Programs, Broken Out by Percentage of Distance Learners Living More than 50 Miles from Campus

Percentage of Distance Learners Living More than 50 Miles from Campus	Yes	No
80-100%	63.64%	36.36%
51-79%	52.94%	47.06%
25-50%	69.57%	30.43%
1-24%	75.00%	25.00%

Chapter Six: Staffing

Over 64% of the sample had an official library liaison to the distance learning program. There was no significant difference in the data reported by U.S. and non-U.S. survey participants. Almost 73% of research universities had an official library liaison to the distance learning programs, compared to just 53% of community colleges, 62.5% of four-year degree-granting colleges, and almost 69% for doctoral level colleges. Public colleges were more likely than private colleges to have a library liaison to the distance learning program; 66% of public colleges and almost 58% of private colleges did so.

The largest colleges were modestly more likely to have a liaison to the distance learning program. While 76% of the largest colleges, with over 12,000 FTE students, had an official library liaison to the distance learning program, 56% of colleges with between 6,001 and 12,000 FTE students had a liaison, as did 60% of colleges with between 2,500 and 6,000 FTE students and 62.5% of colleges with fewer than 2,500 FTE students.

78% of colleges with over 2,000 FTE distance learners had a liaison to the distance learning program, compared with 68.4% of colleges with between 1,000 to 2,000 FTE distance learners and 71% of colleges with fewer than 250 FTE distance learners. Similarly, there was no direct relationship between proportion of distance learners living more than 50 miles from campus and the presence of a library liaison to the distance learning program, but all groups reported uniformly high percentages except for those colleges with 25 to 50% of their distance learners living more than 50 miles away. Just 56.5% of that group had such a liaison, compared to 65% of colleges with fewer than 24% of their distance learners living more than 50 miles away and approximately 70% of colleges with more than 50% of their distance learners living more than 50 miles from campus.

A third of the sample reported that they have a full-time position largely devoted to providing library services to distance learners. Over 42% of non-U.S. libraries have such a position, compared to just 31% of U.S. libraries. Half of all four-year degree-granting colleges had this full-time position for distance learners, while 43% of MA or PhD-granting colleges and 41% of research universities reported similarly. However, barely 15% of community colleges had such a position.

There was little difference between public and private colleges; 33% of public colleges and 35% of private colleges had a full-time position dedicated to distance learning. Nearly half, 48%, of colleges with over 12,000 FTE students had such a position, compared to just 28% of colleges with between 2,500 and 12,000 FTE students, and 29% of colleges with fewer than 2,500 FTE students. Half of all colleges with over 2,000 FTE distance learners had a full-time library position for distance learners, while almost 53% of colleges with between 1,000 and 2,000 FTE distance learners reported the same. Colleges with fewer FTE distance learners were less likely to have a full-time position devoted to distance learning students; just 25% of colleges with between 250 and 999 FTE distance learners and 14% of colleges with fewer than 250 FTE distance learners had this position. As the proportion of distance learners living more than 50 miles from campus increased, so too did the likelihood that the library had a full-time position dedicated to the needs of distance learning students. As much as 48% of colleges with over 80% of their distance learners living more than 50 miles away had such a program, compared to 41% of colleges with between 51 and 79% of their distance learners living more than 50 miles away, and 30% of colleges with fewer than 50% of their distance learners living more than 50 miles away.

The mean number of library FTE staff devoted specifically to the needs of distance learners was 1.36, with a median of 1 and a maximum of 12.5. Non-U.S. libraries had a mean of 1.59 and median of 1.5 FTE positions, compared with a mean of 1.29 and median of 1 reported by U.S. libraries. Community colleges reported the smallest mean at 1.02, while research universities reported the highest number, a mean of 1.75. Four-year degree-granting colleges and MA or PhD-granting colleges were in between at 1.33 and 1.23 mean FTE positions, respectively.

The median for all Carnegie classes was 1. Public colleges reported an average of .32 more FTE positions dedicated to distance learners, compared to private colleges. Colleges with between 6,001 and 12,000 FTE students had a mean of 2.11 FTE positions dedicated to distance learners, while colleges with over 12,000 FTE students had a mean of 1.37 FTE positions. Colleges with between 2,500 and 6,000 FTE students reported a mean of 1.12, while colleges with fewer than 2,500 FTE students reported a mean of just 0.73 FTE positions. Unsurprisingly, the number of library FTE positions dedicated to the needs of distance learners increased as the number of FTE distance learners increased. Colleges with over 2,000 FTE distance learners had a mean of 2.33 library FTE positions. By comparison, colleges with between 1,000 and 2,000 FTE distance learners had a mean of 1.33, colleges with between 250 and 999 FTE distance learners had a mean of 1.2, and colleges with under 250 FTE distance learners had a mean of .64 FTE positions.

There was no direct correlation between the percentage of distance learners living more than 50 miles away with the size of the FTE staff dedicated to the needs of distance learners. Colleges with over 80% of their distance learners living more than 50 miles from campus reported a mean of 1.52 FTE staff, while colleges with between 51 and 79% of their distance learners living more than 50 miles from campus reported a mean of 2. Colleges with between 25 and 50% of their distance learners living more than 50 miles from campus reporet a mean of 1.09 FTE positions, while colleges with fewer than 24% of their distance learners living more than 50 miles away reported a mean of just .96 FTE staff.

Just over 11% of the sample had a specific disbursement or line item in the library budget for distance learning programs. The vast majority did not appear to break down their library budget in this way. Nearly 16% of non-U.S. libraries had a specific disbursement or line item in the library budget for distance learning programs, compared to 10% of U.S. libraries. Over 27% of research universities had such a disbursement or line item for distance learning programs, but this is far higher than any other Carnegie class reported. Just 8.8% of community colleges, 5.9% of MA or PhD-granting colleges, and no four-year degree-granting colleges in our sample reported the same. Public colleges were over 3 times more likely than private colleges to have a specific disbursement or line item for the distance learning program budget. Almost 14% of public colleges had such a disbursement or line item, compared to just 4% of private colleges. Nearly 21% of colleges with over 12,000 FTE students also reported the same, compared to 8% of colleges with fewer than 12,000 FTE students. In general, the likelihood of libraries having a specific disbursement or line item in the library budget for distance learning programs increased as the number of FTE distance learning students increased. As high as 29% of colleges with over 2,000 FTE distance learners had such a disbursement or line item, compared to under 16% of colleges with between 1,000 and 2,000 FTE distance learners, 5% of colleges between 250 and 999 FTE distance learners, and 4.8% of colleges with fewer than 250 FTE distance learners.

There also appeared to be a correlation between disbursement or line item budgeting for distance learning programs and whether the distance learning students living more than 50 miles away comprised more or less than 50% of the distance learning population. Between 17 and 18.75% of colleges with over 50% of their distance learners living more than 50 miles from campus had such a disbursement or line item for distance learning programs. However, between 4.25 and 5% of colleges with fewer than 50% of their distance learners living more than 50 miles from campus reported the same.

Table 6.1:   Percentage of Libraries that have an Official Liaison to the Distance Learning Program

	Yes	No
Entire Sample	63.64%	36.36%

Table 6.2:   Percentage of Libraries that have an Official Liaison to the Distance Learning Program, Broken Out by U.S. and Non-U.S. Libraries

U.S. and Non-U.S. Libraries	Yes	No
U.S.	63.75%	36.25%
Non-U.S.	63.16%	36.84%

Table 6.3:   Percentage of Libraries that have an Official Liaison to the Distance Learning Program, Broken Out by Carnegie Class

Carnegie Class	Yes	No
Community College	52.94%	47.06%
4-Year Degree Granting College	62.50%	37.50%
MA or PhD Granting College	68.57%	31.43%
Research University	72.73%	27.27%

Table 6.4:   Percentage of Libraries that have an Official Liaison to the Distance Learning Program, Broken Out by Public or Private Status

Public or Private Status	Yes	No
Public College	65.75%	34.25%
Private College	57.69%	42.31%

Table 6.5: Percentage of Libraries that have an Official Liaison to the Distance Learning Program, Broken Out by Number of FTE Students at the Institution

Number of FTE Students at the Institution	Yes	No
>12,000	76.00%	24.00%
6,001-12,000	56.00%	44.00%
2,500-6,000	60.00%	40.00%
<2,500	62.50%	37.50%

Table 6.6: Percentage of Libraries that have an Official Liaison to the Distance Learning Program, Broken Out by Number of FTE Distance Learners

Number of FTE Distance Learners	Yes	No
>2,000	77.78%	22.22%
1,000-2,000	68.42%	31.58%
250-999	45.00%	55.00%
<250	71.43%	28.57%

Table 6.7: Percentage of Libraries that have an Official Liaison to the Distance Learning Program, Broken Out by Percentage of Distance Learners Living More than 50 Miles from Campus

Percentage of Distance Learners Living More than 50 Miles from Campus	Yes	No
80-100%	69.57%	30.43%
51-79%	70.59%	29.41%
25-50%	56.52%	43.48%
1-24%	65.00%	35.00%

Table 6.8: Percentage of Libraries that have a Full Time Position Largely Devoted to Providing Library Services to Distance Learners

	Yes	No
Entire Sample	33.33%	66.67%

Table 6.9: Percentage of Libraries that have a Full Time Position Largely Devoted to Providing Library Services to Distance Learners, Broken Out by U.S. and Non-U.S. Libraries

U.S. and Non-U.S. Libraries	Yes	No
U.S.	31.25%	68.75%
Non-U.S.	42.11%	57.89%

Table 6.10: **Percentage of Libraries that have a Full Time Position Largely Devoted to Providing Library Services to Distance Learners, Broken Out by Carnegie Class**

Carnegie Class	Yes	No
Community College	14.71%	85.29%
4-Year Degree Granting College	50.00%	50.00%
MA or PhD Granting College	42.86%	57.14%
Research University	40.91%	59.09%

Table 6.11: **Percentage of Libraries that have a Full Time Position Largely Devoted to Providing Library Services to Distance Learners, Broken Out by Public or Private Status**

Public or Private Status	Yes	No
Public College	32.88%	67.12%
Private College	34.62%	65.38%

Table 6.12: **Percentage of Libraries that have a Full Time Position Largely Devoted to Providing Library Services to Distance Learners, Broken Out by Number of FTE Students at the Institution**

Number of FTE Students at the Institution	Yes	No
>12,000	48.00%	52.00%
6,001-12,000	28.00%	72.00%
2,500-6,000	28.00%	72.00%
<2,500	29.17%	70.83%

Table 6.13: **Percentage of Libraries that have a Full Time Position Largely Devoted to Providing Library Services to Distance Learners, Broken Out by Number of FTE Distance Learners**

Number of FTE Distance Learners	Yes	No
>2,000	50.00%	50.00%
1,000-2,000	52.63%	47.37%
250-999	25.00%	75.00%
<250	14.29%	85.71%

Table 6.14:   Percentage of Libraries that have a Full Time Position Largely Devoted to Providing Library Services to Distance Learners, Broken Out by Percentage of Distance Learners Living More than 50 Miles from Campus

Percentage of Distance Learners Living More than 50 Miles from Campus	Yes	No
80-100%	47.83%	52.17%
51-79%	41.18%	58.82%
25-50%	30.43%	69.57%
1-24%	30.00%	70.00%

Table 6.15:   Mean, Median, Minimum and Maximum Staff Size in FTE Terms of Libraries that have Specific Staff Devoted to the Needs of Distance Learners

	Mean	Median	Minimum	Maximum
Entire Sample	1.36	1.00	0.00	12.50

Table 6.16:   Mean, Median, Minimum and Maximum Staff Size in FTE Terms of Libraries that have Specific Staff Devoted to the Needs of Distance Learners, Broken Out by U.S. and Non-U.S. Libraries

U.S. and Non-U.S. Libraries	Mean	Median	Minimum	Maximum
U.S.	1.29	1.00	0.00	12.50
Non-U.S.	1.59	1.50	0.20	3.50

Table 6.17:   Mean, Median, Minimum and Maximum Staff Size in FTE Terms of Libraries that have Specific Staff Devoted to the Needs of Distance Learners, Broken Out by Carnegie Class

Carnegie Class	Mean	Median	Minimum	Maximum
Community College	1.02	1.00	0.20	3.00
4-Year Degree Granting College	1.33	1.00	1.00	2.00
MA or PhD Granting College	1.23	1.00	0.00	5.00
Research University	1.75	1.00	0.00	12.50

Table 6.18: Mean, Median, Minimum and Maximum Staff Size in FTE Terms of Libraries that have Specific Staff Devoted to the Needs of Distance Learners, Broken Out by Public or Private Status

Public or Private Status	Mean	Median	Minimum	Maximum
Public College	1.44	1.00	0.10	12.50
Private College	1.12	1.00	0.00	5.00

Table 6.19: Mean, Median, Minimum and Maximum Staff Size in FTE Terms of Libraries that have Specific Staff Devoted to the Needs of Distance Learners, Broken Out by Number of FTE Students at the Institution

Number of FTE Students at the Institution	Mean	Median	Minimum	Maximum
>12,000	1.37	1.00	0.50	3.50
6,001-12,000	2.11	1.00	0.10	12.50
2,500-6,000	1.12	1.00	0.00	3.00
<2,500	0.73	1.00	0.00	1.00

Table 6.20: Mean, Median, Minimum and Maximum Staff Size in FTE Terms of Libraries that have Specific Staff Devoted to the Needs of Distance Learners, Broken Out by Number of FTE Distance Learners

Number of FTE Distance Learners	Mean	Median	Minimum	Maximum
>2,000	2.33	1.00	0.00	12.50
1,000-2,000	1.33	1.00	0.25	3.00
250-999	1.20	1.00	1.00	2.00
<250	0.64	0.50	0.10	1.00

Table 6.21: Mean, Median, Minimum and Maximum Staff Size in FTE Terms of Libraries that have Specific Staff Devoted to the Needs of Distance Learners, Broken Out by Percentage of Distance Learners Living More than 50 Miles from Campus

Percentage of Distance Learners Living More than 50 Miles from Campus	Mean	Median	Minimum	Maximum
80-100%	1.52	1.00	0.20	5.00
51-79%	2.00	1.00	0.00	12.50
25-50%	1.09	1.00	0.50	2.00
1-24%	0.96	1.00	0.10	1.50

Table 6.22: Percentage of Libraries that have a Specific Disbursement or Line Item in the Library Budget for Distance Learning Programs

	Yes	No
Entire Sample	11.22%	88.78%

Table 6.23: Percentage of Libraries that have a Specific Disbursement or Line Item in the Library Budget for Distance Learning Programs, Broken Out by U.S. and Non-U.S. Libraries

U.S. and Non-U.S. Libraries	Yes	No
U.S.	10.13%	89.87%
Non-U.S.	15.79%	84.21%

Table 6.24: Percentage of Libraries that have a Specific Disbursement or Line Item in the Library Budget for Distance Learning Programs, Broken Out by Carnegie Class

Carnegie Class	Yes	No
Community College	8.82%	91.18%
4-Year Degree Granting College	0.00%	100.00%
MA or PhD Granting College	5.88%	94.12%
Research University	27.27%	72.73%

Table 6.25: Percentage of Libraries that have a Specific Disbursement or Line Item in the Library Budget for Distance Learning Programs, Broken Out by Public or Private Status

Public or Private Status	Yes	No
Public College	13.70%	86.30%
Private College	4.00%	96.00%

Table 6.26: Percentage of Libraries that have a Specific Disbursement or Line Item in the Library Budget for Distance Learning Programs, Broken Out by Number of FTE Students at the Institution

Number of FTE Students at the Institution	Yes	No
>12,000	20.83%	79.17%
6,001-12,000	8.00%	92.00%
2,500-6,000	8.00%	92.00%
<2,500	8.33%	91.67%

Table 6.27:   Percentage of Libraries that have a Specific Disbursement or Line Item in the Library Budget for Distance Learning Programs, Broken Out by Number of FTE Distance Learners

Number of FTE Distance Learners	Yes	No
>2,000	29.41%	70.59%
1,000-2.000	15.79%	84.21%
250-999	5.00%	95.00%
<250	4.76%	95.24%

Table 6.28:   Percentage of Libraries that have a Specific Disbursement or Line Item in the Library Budget for Distance Learning Programs, Broken Out by Percentage of Distance Learners Living More than 50 Miles from Campus

Percentage of Distance Learners Living More than 50 Miles from Campus	Yes	No
80-100%	17.39%	82.61%
51-79%	18.75%	81.25%
25-50%	4.35%	95.65%
1-24%	5.00%	95.00%

Chapter Seven: Assessment

Over 23% of the sample had ever administered a questionnaire to distance learners to assess their skill in using the library. While almost 39% of non-U.S. libraries reported conducting such a study, just 20% of U.S. libraries did. Over 37% of four-year degree-granting colleges conducted such surveys, while just under 26% of MA or PhD-granting colleges, 23% of research universities, and under 18% of community colleges have done so. Almost a quarter of the public colleges and just 19% of private colleges have conducted assessment surveys of distance learning students' use of library services. 32% of colleges with between 2,500 and 6,000 FTE students had administered such a questionnaire, as had 28% of colleges with over 12,000 FTE students. Just 16% of colleges with between 6,001 and 12,000 FTE students and colleges with under 2,500 FTE students reported the same.

Just over 30% of of the sample believed that they had not done much to cater to their distance learners, and should be doing much more. Another 38% reported that they had done a fair amount but should be doing more. Another 27% reported that they had made a significant effort to cater to distance learning students, and just 4% assessed themselves as having done quite well in dealing with distance learners. Non-U.S. respondents were more likely than U.S. participants to indicate that more needed to be done, but also that they considered themselves to have already done quite well. U.S. institutions were more likely than non-U.S. libraries to believe they had made a significant effort to cater to distance learning students. Community colleges were the most negative in their self-assessment; barely 3% believed themselves to be dealing well with the issue, and under 9% believed they had made a significant effort already to cater to distance learners. Over 41% of community colleges reported they had not done much and should be doing more, while another 47% felt they had done a fair amount but still needed to do more.

Over 42% of private colleges felt they had already made a significant effort to cater to distance learning students, while only 22% of public colleges indicated the same. Private colleges seemed overall more satisfied with their progress and efforts to cater to distance learning students. Over 41% of public colleges reported that they had done a fair amount but should be doing more, compared to 31% of private colleges; almost 33% of public colleges and 23% of private colleges reported that they had not done much but should be doing more. Colleges with over 12,000 FTE students reported the greatest satisfaction in their library's efforts to cater to distance learners, with 44% reporting that they had made a significant effort already. By comparison, 32% of colleges with between 2,500 and 6,000 FTE students reported the same, while just 16% of colleges with fewer than 2,500 FTE students or between 6,001 and 12,000 FTE students reported that they had made a significant effort. Instead, the latter group reported that they had done a fair amount but should be doing more; 44% of the colleges with 6,001 to 12,000 FTE students and 50% of the colleges with fewer than 2,500 FTE students assessed their library's efforts as such. Institutions with between 250 and 999 FTE distance learners appeared to be the least satisfied with their efforts to cater to distance learning students; only 15% had made significant efforts, while just 5% had done quite well. Fully half of these colleges reported not having done much but should be doing more, and another 30% had done a fair amount but still should be doing more.

Institutions with fewer than 250 FTE distance learners also reported relatively low satisfaction; barely 29% had made a significant effort, but none had done well with catering to distance learners. Instead, a third had not done much and another 38% had not done much but should be doing more. Institutions with more than 2,000 FTE distance learners reported relatively high satisfaction with their efforts, with almost 39% indicating that they have made a significant effort already and another 5.6% reporting that they had done quite well already.

The higher the proportion of distance learning students living over 50 miles away, the more satisfied participants reported to be with their library's efforts to cater to distance learning students. Of the colleges with over 80% of their distance learners living more than 50 miles away, over 39% reported already having made a significant effort and another 8.7% that they had done quite well. Just 13% reported that they had not done much and should be doing more, while the remainder, 39%, reported they had done a fair amount but should be doing more. By comparison, just 20% of the colleges with fewer than 24% of their distance learners living more than 50 miles away reported they they had made a significant effort already, and none reported that they were doing quite well. Rather, half reported that they had done a fair amount but needed to do more, while 30% reported that they had not done much at all but needed to do more.

The majority of the libraries in the sample, over 82%, reported that their college's distance learners' level of information literacy was on par with that of traditional students. Just 13% reported that distance learners' skill level was on average lower than traditional students', and just over 4% reported that it was higher than traditional students' skill levels. Non-U.S. colleges were 3 times more likely to report that their distance learners' information literacy skills were lower than that of their traditional students', 29.4% compared to the 9.5% of U.S. institutions. Additionally, no non-U.S. participant reported that their distance learners had a higher skill level than their traditional students, while 5.4% of U.S. institutions did. Research universities, at almost 29%, were much more likely to report that their distance learners had a lower skill level than their traditional counterparts. By comparison, nearly 17% of four-year degree-granting colleges, 9% of MA or PhD-granting colleges, and under 7% of community colleges reported that their distance learners' information literacy skills were lower than that of traditional students'. In fact, no research university and no four-year degree-granting college reported that their distance learners' information literacy skills were higher than that of traditional students'. Nine out of 10 community colleges, the most of any Carnegie class, reported that distance learning and traditional students had the same level of information literacy skills.

Public colleges were almost 4 times more likely than private colleges to assess their distance learners' information literacy skill level to be lower than that of traditional students', while private colleges were almost 9 times more likely than public colleges to assess their distance learners' skill levels to be higher than that of their traditional students'. No institutions with more than 6,001 FTE students reported that their distance learners' information literacy skill level was higher than that of their traditional students, though 12% of institutions with between 2,500 and 6,000 FTE students and over 4% of colleges with fewer than 2,500 FTE students reported that their distance learners' skill level was in fact higher than traditional students. Institutions with between 2,500 and 6,000 FTE students were least likely to consider distance learners and traditional students' skill levels to be on par, with just 68% reporting as such and 20% reporting that distance learners had a lower skill level than traditional students when it came to information literacy. No institutions with between 250 and 2,000 FTE distance learners reported that their distance learners' skill level was higher than that of their traditional students, although 11% of institutions with fewer than 250 FTE distance learners and almost 6% of institutions with over 2,000 FTE distance learners reported that their distance learners' information literacy skills were in fact higher than their traditional students'.

There was no direct correlation between proportion of distance learners living more than 50 miles away and participants' relative assessment of their distance learners' and traditional students' information literacy skills. In fact, no institution with between 51 and 79% of their distance learners living more than 50 miles from campus reported that their distance learners' and traditional students' skills were anything but at the same level. Meanwhile, 65% of colleges with over 80% of their distance learners living more than 50 miles away reported that distance learners and traditional students were on par. In fact, among those colleges, over 30% reported that distance learners were at a lower skill level compared to traditional students, and just over 4% reported that distance learners were at a higher skill level than traditional students. Institutions with between 25 and 50% of their distance learners living more than 50 miles from campus were 3 times as likely to consider that their distance learners' information literacy skill level was lower than that of their traditional students, compared with the 5.6% of institutions with fewer than 24% distance learners living more than 50 miles from campus.

Across the sample, the majority, over 62%, reported that the relationship between the library and the college's distance learning program was about the same as with other administrative or academic departments at the college. Over 13% reported that the library's relationship was perhaps not as good as with other departments at the college, and nearly 24% reported that it was perhaps a little better than relationships with other administrative or academic departments at the college.

U.S. participants were almost 3 times more likely than non-U.S. partaicipants to assess the library's relationship with distance learning departments as not as good as the library's relationship with other departments, but also twice as likely to consider their relationship better than the library's relationships with other departments. Meanwhile, over 82% of non-U.S. respondents indicated that the relationship was roughly the same as it was with other departments; just 58% of U.S. respondents indicated the same. Community colleges, at 30%, were most likely to consider the relationship between the library and distance learning program to be better than the library's relationship with other departments. Next was MA or PhD-granting colleges, almost 23% of whom reported that their relationship was better with the distance learning program than with other departments. Over 19% of research universities reported the same, as did 14% of four-year degree-granting colleges. Research universities, at almost 24%, were most likely to believe that the relationship between the library and distance learning program was not as good as relationships between the library and other departments. Public colleges, compared to private colleges, were more than 60% more likely to indicate that the relationship between the library and the distance learning program was better than that between the library and other departments. Private colleges, in fact, were more likely to believe the relationship between the library and distance learning program to be worse than that with other departments. Institutions with very high or low FTE student enrollments were most likely to indicate that the relationship between the library and distance learning program was better than that with other college departments. However, just 12% of colleges with between 2,500 and 6,000 FTE students reported the relationship to be better than relationships with other department, a drop of over 50% compared to institutions of smaller or larger sizes. Also, no institution between 6,001 and 12,000 FTE students reported that the relationship between the library and distance learning program was worse than that with other departments, compared to 16-17% of institutions with over 12,000 FTE students or between 2,500 and 6,000 FTE students. Almost 22% of institutions with fewer than 2,500 FTE students reported that the library's relationship with the distance learning program was worse than that with other departments.

Curiously, institutions with more than 2,000 FTE distance learners were most likely to indicate that the library-distance learning program relationship was not as good as relationships between the library and other departments within the college. As many as 22% reported the relationship was worse, compared to over 5% of institutions with between 1,000 and 2,000 FTE distance learners and 10% of institutions with fewer than 999 FTE distance learners.

Institutions with fewer than 79% of their distance learners living more than 50 miles from campus were also much more likely to consider the library-distance learning program relationship to be better than relationships between the library and other departments. While just 9% of institutions with more than 80% of their distance learning students living more than 50 miles from campus reported that the relationship was better than that with other departments, institutions with fewer than 80% reported over 3 times that rate. No institution with fewer than 24% of their distance learners living more than 50 miles from campus reported the library-distance learning program relationship to be worse than that between the library and other departments.

Nearly 65% of respondents believe that the library should make a greater effort to serve their distance learning students. Another 34% reported that the library already makes a sufficient effort to serve distances learners. Just over 1% of respondents indicated that the library was exerting too much effort in serving distance learning students and that those resources might best be put elsewhere. U.S. respondents were over 75% more likely than non-U.S. respondents to believe that the library makes a sufficient effort already to serve distance learning students. No non-U.S. participant indicated that the library exerted too much effort to serve distance learners, compared to 1.28% of the U.S. respondents. The only Carnegie class to report that the library was exerting too much effort, in fact, were four-year degree-granting colleges, which were also most likely to consider that they were already making sufficient efforts to serve distance learners.

Community colleges appeared to be the least satisfied with the library's efforts to serve distance learning students, with over 81% reporting that the library should be making greater efforts. By comparison, just 68% of research universities, 54% of MA of PhD-granting colleges, and 37.5% of four-year degree-granting colleges reported the same. While half of private colleges reported that their library made sufficient efforts to serve distance learners, barely 29% of public colleges indicated the same. Almost 72% of public colleges indicated greater efforts should be made by the library to serve distance learners, compared to just 46% of private colleges. No public college believed the library exerted too much effort in serving distance learners, while almost 4% of private colleges reported that the library's resources would be better spent elsewhere.

There was no linear relationship between FTE student enrollment and participants' assessment of the library's efforts to serve distance learners. In fact, there was little variation for each category of institution according to total attendance.

Roughly twice as many libraries believed that the library should make a greater effort as libraries who believed they already make a sufficient effort to serve distance learners. The only library institution size category to indicate that the library was exerting too much energy on distance learners was institutions with over 12,000 FTE students.

Just a quarter of institutions with between 250 and 999 FTE distance learners believe that the library was making sufficient efforts to serve distance learners, compared to 38% of institutions with fewer than 250 FTE distance learners, 42% of institutions with between 1,000 and 2,000 FTE distance learners, and 44% of distance learners with over 2,000 FTE distance learners.

We asked participants whether they kept any special statistics for distance learning students in order to ascertain how much they use the libraray and its resources and how that use compared to that of traditional students. Many did not have a way to track this information, because distance learning students are not separated from traditional students. Statistics that are pulled, from the proxy server to course management software, are not broken out into such categories. Those respondents who did keep statistics often did so by tracking document delivery statistics, information on library materials mailed out, and by keeping track of consultations with distance learning students through the normal venues: email, chat, phone, etc.

Just 8% of the sample, all of whom were U.S. respondents, had conducted a formal assessment on the reference needs of specifically distance learners. Over 12% of four-year degree granting colleges and 11% of MA or PhD-granting colleges conducted such a study, compared to under 6% of community college and under 5% of research universities. With over 11.54% of private colleges responding that they had conducted such an assessment, private colleges were almost 70% more likely than public colleges to have conducted such a study. A minority of all school sizes responded to this question, with the most responses (16%) from colleges with between 2,500 and 6,000 FTE students and (8%) from colleges with over 12,000 FTE students. Just 4% of colleges with between 6,001 and 12,000 FTE students or fewer than 2,500 FTE students reported the same.

In general, colleges with more FTE distance learners were more likely to have conducted a formal assessment on distance learners' reference needs, though almost 16% of colleges with between 1,000 and 2,000 FTE distance learners responded, compared to just 11% of colleges with over 2,000 FTE distance learners. Just 5% of institutions with fewer than 999 FTE distance learners reported similarly. As much as 20% of respondents whose students living more than 50 miles from campus comprise less than 24% of their distance learners had conducted a formal assessment on distance learners' reference needs, with between 4.35 and 5.88% of institutions with higher percentages of distance learners living more than 50 miles from campus.

Even fewer survey participants have conducted a formal assessment on the specific information literacy needs of distance learners. Just 6% of the sample had done such an assessment. While 6.25% of U.S. participants had conducted the study, 5.26% of non-U.S. respondents reported the same. No four-year degree-granting college had conducted such an assessment, while 11.43% of MA or PhD-granting colleges reported that they had, as had 2.94% of community colleges and 4.55% of research universities. Private colleges were nearly 3 times as likely as public colleges to have conducted an assessment on distance learners' information literacy needs. No institution with between 6,001 and 12,000 FTE students had such a study, while 12% of institutions with between 2,500 and 6,000 FTE students, over 8% of institutions with fewer than 2,500 FTE students and 4% of institutions with over 12,000 FTE students had conducted a study on the information literacy needs of distance learners. Curiously, no institutions with over 2,000 FTE distance learners had conducted this assessment, while almost 16% of institutions with between 1,000 and 2,000 FTE students, 10% of institutions with between 250 and 999 FTE distance learners, and under 5% of institutions with fewer than 250 FTE distance learners had conducted this assessment.

Although no respondents with between 51 and 79% of their distance learners living more than 50 miles from campus had conducted an information literacy assessment, over 13% of institutions with more than 80% of their distance learners living more than 50 miles from campus, 8.7% of institutions with between 25 and 50% of their distance learners living more than 50 miles from campus, and 5% of institutions with fewer than 24% of their distance learners living more than 50 miles from campus had conducted an assessment.

Just over 10% of the sample had conducted a formal assessment on the electronic reserves needs of distance learning instructors. There was no significant difference between data gathered from U.S. and non-U.S. participants. No community colleges or four-year degree granting colleges had conducted such an assessment with their distance learning instructors, though 17% of MA or PhD granting colleges and 18% of research universities in the sample reported doing so. Private colleges were almost twice as likely as public colleges to have conducted this assessment.

Between 12 and 12.5% of institutions in all FTE enrollment size categories conducted this assessment, except for colleges with between 6,001 and 12,000 FTE students, only 4% of which had done so. There was no significant difference between 10 to 11% rates reported by institutions with varying populations of FTE distance learners except those reported by institutions with fewer than 250 FTE distance learners, over 14% of whom reported conducting the assessment.

Over 28% of the sample had conducted a formal assessment on the distance learning faculty's level of satisfaction with the library. Three in 10 U.S. participants had conducted this assessment, compared to 21% of non-U.S. respondents. Almost 21% of community colleges and under 23% of research universities reported having done this assessment, while over 37% of four-year degree-granting colleges and MA or PhD-granting colleges reported the same. While over 42% of private colleges reported doing this assessment, just over 23% of public colleges reported the same.

Colleges with fewer FTE distance learning students at the institution reported higher percentages that had conducted this survey compared to institutions with over 6,000 FTE students. 32% of institutions with between 2,500 and 6,000 FTE students and 29% of institutions with fewer than 2,500 FTE students had conducted this assessment, compared to 28% of institutions with between 6,001 and 12,000 FTE students and 24% of institutions with over 12,000 FTE students. Forty-seven percent of institutions with between 1,000 and 2,000 FTE distance learning students had conducted this formal assessment on distance learners and/or the faculty's level of satisfaction with the library. Almost 28% of institutions with over 2,000 FTE distance learners, 20% of colleges with between 250 and 999 FTE distance learners, and 33% of institutions with under 250 FTE distance learners had conducted the same assessments.

Institutions appeared most likely to conduct such an assessment when over 80% of their distance learners lived more than 50 miles from campus, with over 43% in this category responding that they had. Three in 10 institutions with below 24% of their distance learners living more than 50 miles from campus reported the same.

Table 7.1:   Percentage of Libraries that have ever Administered a Questionnaire to Distance Learners to Assess Their Skill in Using the Library and their Evaluation of it

	Yes	No
Entire Sample	23.23%	76.77%

Table 7.2:   Percentage of Libraries that have ever Administered a Questionnaire to Distance Learners to Assess Their Skill in Using the Library and their Evaluation of it, Broken Out by U.S. and Non-U.S. Libraries

U.S. and Non-U.S. Libraries	Yes	No
U.S.	20.00%	80.00%
Non-U.S.	36.84%	63.16%

Table 7.3:   Percentage of Libraries that have ever Administered a Questionnaire to Distance Learners to Assess Their Skill in Using the Library and their Evaluation of it, Broken Out by Carnegie Class

Carnegie Class	Yes	No
Community College	17.65%	82.35%
4-Year Degree Granting College	37.50%	62.50%
MA or PhD Granting College	25.71%	74.29%
Research University	22.73%	77.27%

Table 7.4:   Percentage of Libraries that have ever Administered a Questionnaire to Distance Learners to Assess Their Skill in Using the Library and their Evaluation of it, Broken Out by Public or Private Status

Public or Private Status	Yes	No
Public College	24.66%	75.34%
Private College	19.23%	80.77%

Table 7.5: Percentage of Libraries that have ever Administered a Questionnaire to Distance Learners to Assess Their Skill in Using the Library and their Evaluation of it, Broken Out by Number of FTE Students at the Institution

Number of FTE Students at the Institution	Yes	No
>12,000	28.00%	72.00%
6,001-12,000	16.00%	84.00%
2,500-6,000	32.00%	68.00%
<2,500	16.67%	83.33%

Table 7.6: Percentage of Libraries that have ever Administered a Questionnaire to Distance Learners to Assess Their Skill in Using the Library and their Evaluation of it, Broken Out by Number of FTE Distance Learners

Number of FTE Distance Learners	Yes	No
>2,000	33.33%	66.67%
1,000-2,000	57.89%	42.11%
250-999	25.00%	75.00%
<250	0.00%	100.00%

Table 7.7: Percentage of Libraries that have ever Administered a Questionnaire to Distance Learners to Assess Their Skill in Using the Library and their Evaluation of it, Broken Out by Percentage of Distance Learners Living More than 50 Miles from Campus

Percentage of Distance Learners Living More than 50 Miles from Campus	Yes	No
80-100%	34.78%	65.22%
51-79%	35.29%	64.71%
25-50%	13.04%	86.96%
1-24%	25.00%	75.00%

Table 7.8: Attitude toward the Library's Efforts to Cater to Distance Learners

	We haven't done much and should be doing more.	We have done a fair amount but should be doing more.	We have made a significant effort to cater to distance learning students.	If I do say so myself we have done quite well in dealing with this issue.
Entire Sample	30.30%	38.38%	27.27%	4.04%

Table 7.9: Attitude toward the Library's Efforts to Cater to Distance Learners, Broken Out by U.S. and Non-U.S. Libraries

U.S. and Non-U.S. Libraries	We haven't done much and should be doing more.	We have done a fair amount but should be doing more.	We have made a significant effort to cater to distance learning students.	If I do say so myself we have done quite well in dealing with this issue.
U.S.	30.00%	37.50%	28.75%	3.75%
Non-U.S.	31.58%	42.11%	21.05%	5.26%

Table 7.10: Attitude toward the Library's Efforts to Cater to Distance Learners, Broken Out by Carnegie Class

Carnegie Class	We haven't done much and should be doing more.	We have done a fair amount but should be doing more.	We have made a significant effort to cater to distance learning students.	If I do say so myself we have done quite well in dealing with this issue.
Community College	41.18%	47.06%	8.82%	2.94%
4-Year Degree Granting College	25.00%	25.00%	37.50%	12.50%
MA or PhD Granting College	25.71%	34.29%	37.14%	2.86%
Research University	22.73%	36.36%	36.36%	4.55%

Table 7.11: Attitude toward the Library's Efforts to Cater to Distance Learners, Broken Out by Public or Private Status

Public or Private Status	We haven't done much and should be doing more.	We have done a fair amount but should be doing more.	We have made a significant effort to cater to distance learning students.	If I do say so myself we have done quite well in dealing with this issue.
Public College	32.88%	41.10%	21.92%	4.11%
Private College	23.08%	30.77%	42.31%	3.85%

Table 7.12: Attitude toward the Library's Efforts to Cater to Distance Learners, Broken Out by Number of FTE Students at the Institution

Number of FTE Students at the Institution	We haven't done much and should be doing more.	We have done a fair amount but should be doing more.	We have made a significant effort to cater to distance learning students.	If I do say so myself we have done quite well in dealing with this issue.
>12,000	24.00%	28.00%	44.00%	4.00%
6,001-12,000	36.00%	44.00%	16.00%	4.00%
2,500-6,000	32.00%	32.00%	32.00%	4.00%
<2,500	29.17%	50.00%	16.67%	4.17%

Table 7.13: Attitude toward the Library's Efforts to Cater to Distance Learners, Broken Out by Number of FTE Distance Learners

Number of FTE Distance Learners	We haven't done much and should be doing more.	We have done a fair amount but should be doing more.	We have made a significant effort to cater to distance learning students.	If I do say so myself we have done quite well in dealing with this issue.
>2,000	16.67%	38.89%	38.89%	5.56%
1,000-2,000	15.79%	42.11%	31.58%	10.53%
250-999	50.00%	30.00%	15.00%	5.00%
<250	33.33%	38.10%	28.57%	0.00%

Table 7.14: Attitude toward the Library's Efforts to Cater to Distance Learners, Broken Out by Percentage of Distance Learners Living More than 50 Miles from Campus

Percentage of Distance Learners Living More than 50 Miles from Campus	We haven't done much and should be doing more.	We have done a fair amount but should be doing more.	We have made a significant effort to cater to distance learning students.	If I do say so myself we have done quite well in dealing with this issue.
80-100%	13.04%	39.13%	39.13%	8.70%
51-79%	23.53%	41.18%	29.41%	5.88%
25-50%	43.48%	26.09%	26.09%	4.35%
1-24%	30.00%	50.00%	20.00%	0.00%

Table 7.15:   Assessment of the Information Literacy of the College's Distance Learners vs. Traditional Students

	At a somewhat lower skill level on average than the traditional students when it comes to information literacy.	At about the same level of traditional students when it comes to information literacy.	At a somewhat higher level than the traditional students when it comes to information literacy.
Entire Sample	13.19%	82.42%	4.40%

Table 7.16:   Assessment of the Information Literacy of the College's Distance Learners vs. Traditional Students, Broken Out by U.S. and Non-U.S. Libraries

U.S. and Non-U.S. Libraries	At a somewhat lower skill level on average than the traditional students when it comes to information literacy.	At about the same level of traditional students when it comes to information literacy.	At a somewhat higher level than the traditional students when it comes to information literacy.
U.S.	9.46%	85.14%	5.41%
Non-U.S.	29.41%	70.59%	0.00%

Table 7.17:   Assessment of the Information Literacy of the College's Distance Learners vs. Traditional Students, Broken Out by Carnegie Class

Carnegie Class	At a somewhat lower skill level on average than the traditional students when it comes to information literacy.	At about the same level of traditional students when it comes to information literacy.	At a somewhat higher level than the traditional students when it comes to information literacy.
Community College	6.67%	90.00%	3.33%
4-Year Degree Granting College	16.67%	83.33%	0.00%
MA or PhD Granting College	8.82%	82.35%	8.82%
Research University	28.57%	71.43%	0.00%

Table 7.18:   Assessment of the Information Literacy of the College's Distance Learners vs. Traditional Students, Broken Out by Public or Private Status

Public or Private Status	At a somewhat lower skill level on average than the traditional students when it comes to information literacy.	At about the same level of traditional students when it comes to information literacy.	At a somewhat higher level than the traditional students when it comes to information literacy.
Public College	16.18%	82.35%	1.47%
Private College	4.35%	82.61%	13.04%

Table 7.19: Assessment of the Information Literacy of the College's Distance Learners vs. Traditional Students, Broken Out by Number of FTE Students at the Institution

Number of FTE Students at the Institution	At a somewhat lower skill level on average than the traditional students when it comes to information literacy.	At about the same level of traditional students when it comes to information literacy.	At a somewhat higher level than the traditional students when it comes to information literacy.
>12,000	10.00%	90.00%	0.00%
6,001-12,000	8.70%	91.30%	0.00%
2,500-6,000	20.00%	68.00%	12.00%
<2,500	13.04%	82.61%	4.35%

Table 7.20: Assessment of the Information Literacy of the College's Distance Learners vs. Traditional Students, Broken Out by Number of FTE Distance Learners

Number of FTE Distance Learners	At a somewhat lower skill level on average than the traditional students when it comes to information literacy.	At about the same level of traditional students when it comes to information literacy.	At a somewhat higher level than the traditional students when it comes to information literacy.
>2,000	11.76%	82.35%	5.88%
1,000-2,000	15.79%	84.21%	0.00%
250-999	10.53%	89.47%	0.00%
<250	11.11%	77.78%	11.11%

Table 7.21: Assessment of the Information Literacy of the College's Distance Learners vs. Traditional Students, Broken Out by Percentage of Distance Learners Living More than 50 Miles from Campus

Percentage of Distance Learners Living More than 50 Miles from Campus	At a somewhat lower skill level on average than the traditional students when it comes to information literacy.	At about the same level of traditional students when it comes to information literacy.	At a somewhat higher level than the traditional students when it comes to information literacy.
80-100%	30.43%	65.22%	4.35%
51-79%	0.00%	100.00%	0.00%
25-50%	18.18%	72.73%	9.09%
1-24%	5.56%	88.89%	5.56%

Table 7.22:   Assessment of the Relationship Between the Library and the College's Distance Learning Program

	Perhaps not quite as good as with other administrative and/or academic departments at the college.	About the same as with other administrative and/or academic departments at the college.	Perhaps a little better than with other administrative and/or academic departments at the college.
Entire Sample	13.54%	62.50%	23.96%

Table 7.23:   Assessment of the Relationship Between the Library and the College's Distance Learning Program, Broken Out by U.S. and Non-U.S. Libraries

U.S. and Non-U.S. Libraries	Perhaps not quite as good as with other administrative and/or academic departments at the college.	About the same as with other administrative and/or academic departments at the college.	Perhaps a little better than with other administrative and/or academic departments at the college.
U.S.	15.19%	58.23%	26.58%
Non-U.S.	5.88%	82.35%	11.76%

Table 7.24:   Assessment of the Relationship Between the Library and the College's Distance Learning Program, Broken Out by Carnegie Class

Carnegie Class	Perhaps not quite as good as with other administrative and/or academic departments at the college.	About the same as with other administrative and/or academic departments at the college.	Perhaps a little better than with other administrative and/or academic departments at the college.
Community College	3.03%	66.67%	30.30%
4-Year Degree Granting College	14.29%	71.43%	14.29%
MA or PhD Granting College	17.14%	60.00%	22.86%
Research University	23.81%	57.14%	19.05%

Table 7.25:   Assessment of the Relationship Between the Library and the College's Distance Learning Program, Broken Out by Public or Private Status

Public or Private Status	Perhaps not quite as good as with other administrative and/or academic departments at the college.	About the same as with other administrative and/or academic departments at the college.	Perhaps a little better than with other administrative and/or academic departments at the college.
Public College	12.68%	60.56%	26.76%
Private College	16.00%	68.00%	16.00%

Table 7.26: Assessment of the Relationship Between the Library and the College's Distance Learning Program, Broken Out by Number of FTE Students at the Institution

Number of FTE Students at the Institution	Perhaps not quite as good as with other administrative and/or academic departments at the college.	About the same as with other administrative and/or academic departments at the college.	Perhaps a little better than with other administrative and/or academic departments at the college.
>12,000	16.67%	54.17%	29.17%
6,001-12,000	0.00%	75.00%	25.00%
2,500-6,000	16.00%	72.00%	12.00%
<2,500	21.74%	47.83%	30.43%

Table 7.27: Assessment of the Relationship Between the Library and the College's Distance Learning Program, Broken Out by Number of FTE Distance Learners

Number of FTE Distance Learners	Perhaps not quite as good as with other administrative and/or academic departments at the college.	About the same as with other administrative and/or academic departments at the college.	Perhaps a little better than with other administrative and/or academic departments at the college.
>2,000	22.22%	61.11%	16.67%
1,000-2,000	5.56%	66.67%	27.78%
250-999	10.53%	63.16%	26.32%
<250	10.00%	75.00%	15.00%

Table 7.28: Assessment of the Relationship Between the Library and the College's Distance Learning Program, Broken Out by Percentage of Distance Learners Living More than 50 Miles from Campus

Percentage of Distance Learners Living More than 50 Miles from Campus	Perhaps not quite as good as with other administrative and/or academic departments at the college.	About the same as with other administrative and/or academic departments at the college.	Perhaps a little better than with other administrative and/or academic departments at the college.
80-100%	13.64%	77.27%	9.09%
51-79%	17.65%	52.94%	29.41%
25-50%	13.64%	59.09%	27.27%
1-24%	0.00%	68.42%	31.58%

Table 7.29:   Assessment of the Library's Efforts to Serve Distance Learners

	The library should make a greater effort to serve our distance learning students.	The library makes a sufficient effort to serve our distance learning students.	The library exerts too much effort as it is in serving our distance learning students and resources might best be put elsewhere.
Entire Sample	64.95%	34.02%	1.03%

Table 7.30:   Assessment of the Library's Efforts to Serve Distance Learners, Broken Out by U.S. and Non-U.S. Libraries

U.S. and Non-U.S. Libraries	The library should make a greater effort to serve our distance learning students.	The library makes a sufficient effort to serve our distance learning students.	The library exerts too much effort as it is in serving our distance learning students and resources might best be put elsewhere.
U.S.	61.54%	37.18%	1.28%
Non-U.S.	78.95%	21.05%	0.00%

Table 7.31:   Assessment of the Library's Efforts to Serve Distance Learners, Broken Out by Carnegie Class

Carnegie Class	The library should make a greater effort to serve our distance learning students.	The library makes a sufficient effort to serve our distance learning students.	The library exerts too much effort as it is in serving our distance learning students and resources might best be put elsewhere.
Community College	81.25%	18.75%	0.00%
4-Year Degree Granting College	37.50%	50.00%	12.50%
MA or PhD Granting College	54.29%	45.71%	0.00%
Research University	68.18%	31.82%	0.00%

Table 7.32:   Assessment of the Library's Efforts to Serve Distance Learners, Broken Out by Public or Private Status

Public or Private Status	The library should make a greater effort to serve our distance learning students.	The library makes a sufficient effort to serve our distance learning students.	The library exerts too much effort as it is in serving our distance learning students and resources might best be put elsewhere.
Public College	71.83%	28.17%	0.00%
Private College	46.15%	50.00%	3.85%

Table 7.33:   Assessment of the Library's Efforts to Serve Distance Learners, Broken Out by Number of FTE Students at the Institution

Number of FTE Students at the Institution	The library should make a greater effort to serve our distance learning students.	The library makes a sufficient effort to serve our distance learning students.	The library exerts too much effort as it is in serving our distance learning students and resources might best be put elsewhere.
>12,000	62.50%	33.33%	4.17%
6,001-12,000	70.83%	29.17%	0.00%
2,500-6,000	64.00%	36.00%	0.00%
<2,500	62.50%	37.50%	0.00%

Table 7.34:   Assessment of the Library's Efforts to Serve Distance Learners, Broken Out by Number of FTE Distance Learners

Number of FTE Distance Learners	The library should make a greater effort to serve our distance learning students.	The library makes a sufficient effort to serve our distance learning students.	The library exerts too much effort as it is in serving our distance learning students and resources might best be put elsewhere.
>2,000	55.56%	44.44%	0.00%
1,000-2,000	57.89%	42.11%	0.00%
250-999	75.00%	25.00%	0.00%
<250	61.90%	38.10%	0.00%

Table 7.35:   Assessment of the Library's Efforts to Serve Distance Learners, Broken Out by Percentage of Distance Learners Living More than 50 Miles from Campus

Percentage of Distance Learners Living More than 50 Miles from Campus	The library should make a greater effort to serve our distance learning students.	The library makes a sufficient effort to serve our distance learning students.	The library exerts too much effort as it is in serving our distance learning students and resources might best be put elsewhere.
80-100%	43.48%	56.52%	0.00%
51-79%	58.82%	41.18%	0.00%
25-50%	72.73%	27.27%	0.00%
1-24%	68.42%	31.58%	0.00%

Survey of Library Services for Distance Learning Programs

Answers to the prompt, "If your library keeps any special statistics for distance learning students in order to ascertain how much they use the library and its resources, how does their use compares to that of traditional students, and how they evaluate those resources, please describe these efforts here."

1. The only way that we have to see if distance users are using the library is through the remote access part of EBSCOhost, and even then we don't know who are our distance students and who are just traditional students logging in from home.
2. We track number of requests to use online proprietary resources. Hard to tell, really, because over 70% of our classes make at least some use of course management software.
3. We cannot identify distance learners as a group!
4. We keep statistics on document delivery to distance education students. We can also use ANGEL to see how many students have accessed our library guides and Weblinks.
5. We try to see how many students are enrolled in DE courses. We also keep stats on the number of students who contact us, as well as the number of requests.
6. Distance students are identified as such in our ILLiad database.
7. We keep track of reference question #s and #s of print items requested.
8. The only measurement we keep is how many books and paper articles are requested by distance students. It is impossible to know how many electronic books and e-journals they look at versus on-campus students.
9. We would have circ stats (# of items mailed out to students).
10. We track the number of requests that distant students make to borrow materials from our collection, numbers of requests for copies of articles that we own only in print (we deliver as PDF), and interlibrary loan requests for articles (we don't provide interlibrary loan of books for DE students). We track the number of classes taught, whether a librarian visits a distance ed site in person or works virtually through the BlackBoard course management system. We also count consultations that arise from instruction sessions, and these may take the form of appointments in person, IM sessions, phone conversations, or e-mail exchanges.
11. We don't keep these statistics.
12. We try to track reference services provided to distance students as distinct from general reference; we track instruction and orientation sessions offered.
13. We keep ILL statistics by program and location of requests. We ask subjective questions of education graduate students on how satisfied they are with library services.
14. We have been unable to do much in this direction because most sources which we can get statistics from do not allow us to differentiate between different user groups.
15. Not at this time but we hope to track that through WebCT beginning next fall.
16. I every fully online class that requires library research in which I participate in my librarian role with a discussion board forum; on average less than 50% of the students in each course take advantage of my participation.
17. The coordinator of distance learning includes a question about whether students used the library and if they didn't, why that was the case. Usually the "why" is that they didn't know they could, so we definitely need to get the word out.

18. We keep track of the number and type of questions we get from our distance learning students (and we do the same for our traditional students).
19. Right now, we are collecting statistics from our Ask-a-librarian email service and ask them where they take most of their classes. We also track how many online requests we get for library cards on a monthly basis. (The link for applying online for a library card is located only on the distance services page.)
20. No separate statistics; for our online ref services we can't tell who's distant and who's not.
21. We attempt to keep stats on instruction sessions for DE students and reference questions from DE students. However, they require that the students self-identify, so are conservative at best. We do not compare these results with those of traditional students.
22. Distance education students are not separated for statistics; we try to treat them the same as on-campus students.
23. Since library services for DL students are handled separately from those offered to on-campus students, CMU does not typically gather data for comparison purposes. One exception would be tracking use of electronic resources - this data is tracked separately but considered as a whole since these resources are shared by both library services.
24. We do keep track of off-campus article requests from our paper collections (digitised and emailed), and book loans (via mail).
25. I prepare an annual report detailing distance learning students' use of library resources.
26. We keep stats re: number of sessions taught to distance users, reference transactions, number of items shipped to them from our library's collection, and number of interlibrary loans shipped to them. Students are also asked a few questions about library services in their course evaluation form, but these questions need to be revised.
27. We do not have the kind of contacts with Dist. Ed that allow us to learn these things; I couldn't answer #5 because we have tried but we are rebuffed. We have almost no access to those students.

Table 7.36: Percentage of Libraries that have Conducted a Formal Assessment on the Reference Needs Specifically of Distance Learners

	Yes	No
Entire Sample	8.08%	91.92%

Table 7.37: Percentage of Libraries that have Conducted a Formal Assessment on the Reference Needs Specifically of Distance Learners, Broken Out by U.S. and Non-U.S. Libraries

U.S. and Non-U.S. Libraries	Yes	No
U.S.	10.00%	90.00%
Non-U.S.	0.00%	100.00%

Table 7.38: Percentage of Libraries that have Conducted a Formal Assessment on the Reference Needs Specifically of Distance Learners, Broken Out by Carnegie Class

Carnegie Class	Yes	No
Community College	5.88%	94.12%
4-Year Degree Granting College	12.50%	87.50%
MA or PhD Granting College	11.43%	88.57%
Research University	4.55%	95.45%

Table 7.39: Percentage of Libraries that have Conducted a Formal Assessment on the Reference Needs Specifically of Distance Learners, Broken Out by Public or Private Status

Public or Private Status	Yes	No
Public College	6.85%	93.15%
Private College	11.54%	88.46%

Table 7.40: Percentage of Libraries that have Conducted a Formal Assessment on the Reference Needs Specifically of Distance Learners, Broken Out by Number of FTE Students at the Institution

Number of FTE Students at the Institution	Yes	No
>12,000	8.00%	92.00%
6,001-12,000	4.00%	96.00%
2,500-6,000	16.00%	84.00%
<2,500	4.17%	95.83%

Table 7.41: Percentage of Libraries that have Conducted a Formal Assessment on the Reference Needs Specifically of Distance Learners, Broken Out by Number of FTE Distance Learners

Number of FTE Distance Learners	Yes	No
>2,000	11.11%	88.89%
1,000-2,000	15.79%	84.21%
250-999	5.00%	95.00%
<250	4.76%	95.24%

Table 7.42: Percentage of Libraries that have Conducted a Formal Assessment on the Reference Needs Specifically of Distance Learners, Broken Out by Percentage of Distance Learners Living More than 50 Miles from Campus

Percentage of Distance Learners Living More than 50 Miles from Campus	Yes	No
80-100%	4.35%	95.65%
51-79%	5.88%	94.12%
25-50%	4.35%	95.65%
1-24%	20.00%	80.00%

Table 7.43: Percentage of Libraries that have Conducted a Formal Assessment on the Information Literacy Needs Specifically of Distance Learners

	Yes	No
Entire Sample	6.06%	93.94%

Table 7.44: Percentage of Libraries that have Conducted a Formal Assessment on the Information Literacy Needs Specifically of Distance Learners, Broken Out by U.S. and Non-U.S. Libraries

U.S. and Non-U.S. Libraries	Yes	No
U.S.	6.25%	93.75%
Non-U.S.	5.26%	94.74%

Table 7.45: Percentage of Libraries that have Conducted a Formal Assessment on the Information Literacy Needs Specifically of Distance Learners, Broken Out by Carnegie Class

Carnegie Class	Yes	No
Community College	2.94%	97.06%
4-Year Degree Granting College	0.00%	100.00%
MA or PhD Granting College	11.43%	88.57%
Research University	4.55%	95.45%

Table 7.46: Percentage of Libraries that have Conducted a Formal Assessment on the Information Literacy Needs Specifically of Distance Learners, Broken Out by Public or Private Status

Public or Private Status	Yes	No
Public College	4.11%	95.89%
Private College	11.54%	88.46%

Table 7.47:   Percentage of Libraries that have Conducted a Formal Assessment on the Information Literacy Needs Specifically of Distance Learners, Broken Out by Number of FTE Students at the Institution

Number of FTE Students at the Institution	Yes	No
>12,000	4.00%	96.00%
6,001-12,000	0.00%	100.00%
2,500-6,000	12.00%	88.00%
<2,500	8.33%	91.67%

Table 7.48:   Percentage of Libraries that have Conducted a Formal Assessment on the Information Literacy Needs Specifically of Distance Learners, Broken Out by Number of FTE Distance Learners

Number of FTE Distance Learners	Yes	No
>2,000	0.00%	100.00%
1,000-2,000	15.79%	84.21%
250-999	10.00%	90.00%
<250	4.76%	95.24%

Table 7.49:   Percentage of Libraries that have Conducted a Formal Assessment on the Information Literacy Needs Specifically of Distance Learners, Broken Out by Percentage of Distance Learners Living More than 50 Miles from Campus

Percentage of Distance Learners Living More than 50 Miles from Campus	Yes	No
80-100%	13.04%	86.96%
51-79%	0.00%	100.00%
25-50%	8.70%	91.30%
1-24%	5.00%	95.00%

Table 7.50:   Percentage of Libraries that have Conducted a Formal Assessment on the Electronic Reserves Needs of Distance Learning Instructors

	Yes	No
Entire Sample	10.10%	89.90%

Table 7.51:   Percentage of Libraries that have Conducted a Formal Assessment on the Electronic Reserves Needs of Distance Learning Instructors, Broken Out by U.S. and Non-U.S. Libraries

U.S. and Non-U.S. Libraries	Yes	No
U.S.	10.00%	90.00%
Non-U.S.	10.53%	89.47%

Table 7.52:   Percentage of Libraries that have Conducted a Formal Assessment on the Electronic Reserves Needs of Distance Learning Instructors, Broken Out by Carnegie Class

Carnegie Class	Yes	No
Community College	0.00%	100.00%
4-Year Degree Granting College	0.00%	100.00%
MA or PhD Granting College	17.14%	82.86%
Research University	18.18%	81.82%

Table 7.53:   Percentage of Libraries that have Conducted a Formal Assessment on the Electronic Reserves Needs of Distance Learning Instructors, Broken Out by Public or Private Status

Public or Private Status	Yes	No
Public College	8.22%	91.78%
Private College	15.38%	84.62%

Table 7.54:   Percentage of Libraries that have Conducted a Formal Assessment on the Electronic Reserves Needs of Distance Learning Instructors, Broken Out by Number of FTE Students at the Institution

Number of FTE Students at the Institution	Yes	No
>12,000	12.00%	88.00%
6,001-12,000	4.00%	96.00%
2,500-6,000	12.00%	88.00%
<2,500	12.50%	87.50%

Table 7.55:   Percentage of Libraries that have Conducted a Formal Assessment on the Electronic Reserves Needs of Distance Learning Instructors, Broken Out by Number of FTE Distance Learners

Number of FTE Distance Learners	Yes	No
>2,000	11.11%	88.89%
1,000-2,000	10.53%	89.47%
250-999	10.00%	90.00%
<250	14.29%	85.71%

Table 7.56:   Percentage of Libraries that have Conducted a Formal Assessment on the Electronic Reserves Needs of Distance Learning Instructors, Broken Out by Percentage of Distance Learners Living More than 50 Miles from Campus

Percentage of Distance Learners Living More than 50 Miles from Campus	Yes	No
80-100%	17.39%	82.61%
51-79%	5.88%	94.12%
25-50%	8.70%	91.30%
1-24%	15.00%	85.00%

Table 7.57:   Percentage of Libraries that have Conducted a Formal Assessment on Distance Learners and/or Faculty's Level of Satisfaction with the Library

	Yes	No
Entire Sample	28.28%	71.72%

Table 7.58:   Percentage of Libraries that have Conducted a Formal Assessment on Distance Learners and/or Faculty's Level of Satisfaction with the Library, Broken Out by U.S. and Non-U.S. Libraries

U.S. and Non-U.S. Libraries	Yes	No
U.S.	30.00%	70.00%
Non-U.S.	21.05%	78.95%

Table 7.59:   Percentage of Libraries that have Conducted a Formal Assessment on Distance Learners and/or Faculty's Level of Satisfaction with the Library, Broken Out by Carnegie Class

Carnegie Class	Yes	No
Community College	20.59%	79.41%
4-Year Degree Granting College	37.50%	62.50%
MA or PhD Granting College	37.14%	62.86%
Research University	22.73%	77.27%

Table 7.60:   Percentage of Libraries that have Conducted a Formal Assessment on Distance Learners and/or Faculty's Level of Satisfaction with the Library, Broken Out by Public or Private Status

Public or Private Status	Yes	No
Public College	23.29%	76.71%
Private College	42.31%	57.69%

Table 7.61: Percentage of Libraries that have Conducted a Formal Assessment on Distance Learners and/or Faculty's Level of Satisfaction with the Library, Broken Out by Number of FTE Students at the Institution

Number of FTE Students at the Institution	Yes	No
>12,000	24.00%	76.00%
6,001-12,000	28.00%	72.00%
2,500-6,000	32.00%	68.00%
<2,500	29.17%	70.83%

Table 7.62: Percentage of Libraries that have Conducted a Formal Assessment on Distance Learners and/or Faculty's Level of Satisfaction with the Library, Broken Out by Number of FTE Distance Learners

Number of FTE Distance Learners	Yes	No
>2,000	27.78%	72.22%
1,000-2,000	47.37%	52.63%
250-999	20.00%	80.00%
<250	33.33%	66.67%

Table 7.63: Percentage of Libraries that have Conducted a Formal Assessment on Distance Learners and/or Faculty's Level of Satisfaction with the Library, Broken Out by Percentage of Distance Learners Living More than 50 Miles from Campus

Percentage of Distance Learners Living More than 50 Miles from Campus	Yes	No
80-100%	43.48%	56.52%
51-79%	29.41%	70.59%
25-50%	26.09%	73.91%
1-24%	30.00%	70.00%

Chapter Eight: Collection Development

We asked participants how the development of their college's distance learning program has impacted the collection development strategy of the library. The responses of those who reported any impact at all indicate that they increasingly prefer online resources, such as ebooks and databases, over traditional resources. Some reported going beyond preference for online and electronic resources; one participant reported that their collection was entirely made of online resources and would not even be in existence without a distance learning program. Another participant reported that everything bought now is electronic and that they have recently stopped providing physical books through their document delivery system. Participants also are working on increasing off-campus access through proxy servers and remote authentication. Some reported little to no impact of distance learners on the library's collection development, sometimes because the distance learning program is so small, or because the library has moved more towards e-resource as a general policy.

The mean shipping costs accrued annually by sending physical books, magazines and other educational materials to distance learners was $2,048, with a median of $75 and maximum of $19,850. Non-U.S. institutions reported a mean more than 5 times higher than that of U.S. institutions, $5,381 to $1,096. The least was spent by community colleges, just over $267 yearly on shipping costs, while four-year degree-granting colleges reported a mean of $6,666. Research universities reported mean, annual shipping costs of $5,093, while MA or PhD-granting colleges reported a mean of $1,054. Public colleges spent an average of $2,606, compared to just $781 by private colleges.

It should be noted, however, that their medians were much closer, 100 and 50, respectively. Institutions with more than 12,000 FTE students reported a mean of $3,564, while institutions with fewer than 12,000 FTE students reported under $1,950. The lowest amount spent was by institutions with fewer than 2,500 FTE students, who reported spending $1,309 yearly. There was a direct relationship between amount spent annually on shipping costs to send educational materials to distance learners and the number of FTE distance learners. In fact, institutions with over 2,000 FTE distance learners reported a mean of $6,587 and median of $3,250. Institutions with between 1,000 and 2,000 FTE distance learners reported a mean of $2,645 and median of $475. Colleges with between 250 and 999 FTE distance learners reported a mean of $1,383 and median of 50. Those with fewer than 250 FTE distance learning students reported a mean of $221 and median of $50. Institutions whose distance learners living more than 50 miles from campus comprised between 51 and 79% reported a relatively high mean of $7,283 and median of $2,000, whereas institutions whose distance learners living more than 50 miles from campus comprised between 25 and 50% of the distance learners reported a mean of $2,327 and a median of $100.

Over 58% of the sample reported that their usual method of shipping books and other documents to distance learners was through the U.S. Postal Service. Just 1.27% reported that they used certified U.S. mail. Over 24% reported using UPS or another commercial shipper, and over 16% reported using the official state mail service of a country other than the U.S. In fact, over 74% of U.S. respondents reported using U.S. mail with just 1.6% using certified U.S. mail. Just over 76% of non-U.S. respondents reported using their official country's mail service. Just under a quarter of respondents, both U.S. and non-U.S., reported using UPS or another commercial shipper. Just 3.23% of MA or PhD-granting colleges were the only respondents to report using U.S. certified mail. Approximately 75% of all respondents used government mail, with the remainder using commercial shippers, with the exception of four-year degree-granting colleges, only 17% of whom reported using commercial shippers. One-third of these colleges used their non-U.S. government mail, while half used U.S. mail. Private colleges used commercial shippers significantly more than public colleges did; 20% of public colleges used commercial shippers, compared to 35% of private colleges. The remainder used government mail. Commercial shippers were generally more popular with schools with larger FTE enrollments than those with smaller FTE enrollments. Fully 33% of colleges with over 12,000 FTE students reported using primarily commercial shippers, compared to 28% of institutions with 2,500 to 6,000 FTE students, 21% of institutions with 6,001 to 12,000 FTE students, and 16% of institutions with fewer than 2,500 FTE students. Use of commercial shippers also increased considerably as the number of FTE distance learners decreased. In fact, for institutions with over 1,000 FTE distance learners, no more than 15% of the respondents used commercial shippers as their primary method of shipment. Meanwhile, almost 27% of institutions with between 250 and 999 FTE distance learners and a whopping 42% of institutions with fewer than 250 FTE distance learners reported using UPS or other commercial shippers. The only institutions to report using certified U.S. mail were ones with over 2,000 FTE distance learners. Institutions whose students living more than 50 miles from campus comprised more than 80% or less than 24% of the distance learning students reported the highest percentages of using commercial shipping, 35 and 33% respectively. Almost 27% of institutions whose distance learning students living more than 50 miles comprised between 51 and 79% of their distance learners and 15% of the institutions whose distance learners living more than 50 miles from campus comprised between 25 and 50% of the distance learners reported using commercial shippers.

The majority of the sample, over 77%, reported that the library's interlibrary loan staff wasn't responsible for satisfying distance learners' requests for physical copies of books or articles from the library. Another 14% reported that this was the responsibility of the library's distance learning staff, while just over 8% reported that this was part of the job responsibility of another department within the library. Non-U.S. respondents were 3 times more likely to report that satisfying these requests for physical copies of library materials was the responsibility of the library's distance learning staff, compared to U.S. respondents. Non-U.S. respondents were also much more likely to report that another department in the library was in charge of such things; over 23% of non-U.S. respondents reported that another library department was in charge of this, compared to just 4.5% of U.S. respondents. Almost 83% of community colleges and over 78% of MA or PhD-granting colleges reported that the library's interlibrary loan staff was in charge of fulfillment, while four-year degree-granting colleges and research universities both reported that approximately 72% of them had the interlibrary loan staff satisfy the distance learners' needs. Public colleges were almost twice as likely as private colleges to have the library's distance learning staff fulfill requests for physical library materials, making private colleges (82%) more likely than public colleges (76%) to use the interlibrary loan staff to satisfy such requests. Institutions with mid-sized FTE enrollments, between 2,500 and 12,000, reported relatively high percentages having some other library department fulfilling these requests, over 10%. Just 5% of institutions with more than 12,000 or fewer than 2,500 FTE enrollments reported the same. Three in 10 colleges with over 12,000 FTE students, however, reported that the library's distance learning staff was in charge of these fulfillments, compared to just 15% of institutions with between 2,500 and 6,000 FTE students, 8% of institutions with between 6,001 and 12,000 FTE students, and just 5% of those with fewer than 2,500 FTE students. Colleges with the highest number of FTE distance learners, over 2,000, reported that 37.5% of them had the library's distance learning staff handle these requests, 62.5% had their interlibrary loan staff handle them, and none reported using another department. Colleges with fewer FTE distance learners were more likely to use the library's interlibrary loan staff to handle distance learning students' requests for physical materials from the library. Almost 7% of colleges with between 1,000 and 2,000 FTE distance learners used the distance learning staff at the library to fulfill requests, and over 13% reported that another library department handled them. No institution with between 250 and 999 FTE distance learners reported using the distance learning staff at that library, and 6.7% reported using another department. An even 15% of institutions with fewer than 250 FTE distance learners reported using the library's distance learning staff for such fulfillment, and another 10% reported using some other department within the library. The higher the proportion of distance learners living more than 50 miles from campus, the more likely the fulfillments of these requests are handled by the library's distance learning staff, according to the data. As high as 30% of institutions whose distance learners living more than 50 miles from campus comprising more than 80% of their distance learners reported this, compared to 18.75% of institutions in the next tier, whose distance learners living more than 50 miles away comprised 51 to 79% of the distance learners, 5% of institutions whose distance learners living more than 50 miles away comprised between 25 and 50% of the distance learners, and none of the institutions whose distance learners living more than 50 miles away comprised less than 24% of the distance learning students. In fact, institutions whose distance learners living so far away comprised less than 24% of the total distance learners reported that 100% of such requests are fulfilled by interlibrary loan staff. Six to 10% of institutions with higher proportions of distance learners living more than 50 miles away reported using another library department to fulfill these requests.

Just over half of the sample, over 52%, reported that they had no restrictions on the delivery of books, articles and other paper versions of intellectual property to distance learners, meaning that they deliver such materials even if the students live close to campus. Almost 36% reported that they delivered materials only if they live a certain distance away from campus, while 11% reported that the delivery of books only goes to satellite sites from which students can pick up the books. There was little difference between the data gathered from U.S. and non-U.S. participants except that U.S. libraries were twice as likely as non-U.S. libraries to send materials only to satellite sites for students to pick up. Community colleges were least likely to not restrict where they might send library materials, only half of whom will send materials to students no matter where they live. MA or PhD-granting colleges were next at almost 52%, while over 57% of both four-year degree-granting colleges and research universities reported not putting restrictions on the sending of materials. Almost 32% of community colleges and 33% of research universities reported only sending materials if the distance learning students lived a specified distance away from campus, while almost 39% of MA or PhD-granting colleges and nearly 43% of four-year degree granting colleges reported the same. No four-year degree-granting college reported that they only send books to satellite sites that students must pick up materials from, while as much as 18% of community colleges reported using this system. By comparison, almost 10% of MA or PhD-granting colleges and research universities reported sending materials only to satellite sites for pickup. There was little difference between public and private colleges' restrictions on sending library materials to distance learning students, but public colleges were slightly more likely to not put restrictions on sending materials, and less likely to send materials exclusively to satellite sites for students to pick up. Colleges with over 6,001 FTE students were more likely to only deliver books to distance learners living a certain distance away from campus. Four of 10 colleges with over 12,000 FTE students and five out of 10 colleges with between 6,001 and 12,000 FTE students reported that they restricted delivery of library materials in this way, compared to just 21% of colleges with between 2,500 and 6,000 FTE students and 28% of colleges with fewer than 2,500 FTE students. Over 21% of institutions with between 2,500 and 6,000 FTE students, the highest percentage reported, use the satellite system and only send books to sites where students can pick up the materials. Two in three colleges with between 1,000 and 2,000 FTE distance learners reported not restricting the delivery of library materials, while 53% of institutions with over 2,000 FTE distance learners, 40% of institutions with between 250 and 999 distance learners, and 50% of institutions with under 250 distance learners reported the same. Rather, as the number of FTE distance learners decreased, the use of the satellite system increased: as low as 6.67% in institutions with over 1,000 FTE distance learners and as high as 15% in institutions with fewer than 250 FTE distance learners. There was no direct relationship between the proportion of distance learners living more than 50 miles away and restrictions on the delivery of library materials to students, except that as the proportion grew smaller, the use of satellite sites to deliver books increased. As few as 5% of the institutions with the highest percentage of distance learners living more than 50 miles from campus reported using the satellite system, compared with 18.75% of institutions with the lowest percentages of distance learners more than 50 miles from campus.

The vast majority of the sample, close to 89%, reported that the cost of shipping library materials to distance learners was generally paid for by the library. Over 7% reported that the costs are covered by the student, while close to 4% reported that costs are covered by the student through a special fee, regardless of the number of items shipped. This last option was popular with close to 6% of non-U.S. respondents, while chosen only among 3% of U.S. participants. For U.S. participants, costs are more often paid for by the student (7.8%) than with non-U.S. participants (5.9%). Each Carnegie class reported that 86 to 93% of them had the library pay for shipping library materials, except for four-year degree-granting colleges, only 71% of whom reported paying for it through the library. Instead, another 14.3% of them reported that the student paid for shipping fees, and another 14.3% reported that it was a special flat fee paid by the student, regardless of the number of items shipped. Private colleges were over 6 times more likely than public colleges to use this flat fee paid by the student, and also more likely to have the student pay the full amount of the shipping fees, 10% to public colleges' 6.6%. Institutions used the flat fee paid by the student more often as the number of FTE students at the institution decreased; no institution with over 12,000 FTE students reported using this practice, while 5.26% of institutions with fewer than 6,000 FTE students did. Colleges with higher enrollments generally had the library pay for such shipping fees. The same is not true of institutions with increasingly large FTE distance learners, however; colleges with over 2,000 or under FTE distance learners reported that just 82-83% of them had the library cover shipping costs, while 100% of institutions with between 250 and 2,000 FTE distance learners reported that such costs were covered by the library. Instead, 5.9% of institutions with the most distance learners reported that the student bore the costs and 11.8% reported that the costs were covered by a special flat fee, paid by the student. Institutions with the smallest number of FTE distance learners were more likely to have the student cover the full cost (11%) and less likely to have the flat fee charged to the student (5.6%). No institution with fewer than 24% of their distance learners living more than 50 miles from campus reported that they had the students cover the costs of shipping at all. However, almost 95% of institutions with more than 80% of their distance learners living more than 50 miles away also reported that the library covered such costs, with the remainder, 5.3%, reporting that the costs are covered by the student. Just eight in 10 institutions with between 25 and 79% of their distance learners living more than 50 miles away were likely to report that the library covered the shipping costs, with the remainder being covered by the student through full or flat fees.

Answers to the prompt, "How has the development of your college's distance learning program impacted the collection development strategy of your library?"

1. We tend to be focusing our efforts more on buying online databases than traditional books because we are aware that many students cannot come to the physical library.
2. We prefer online resources now, especially periodicals.
3. Yes! We were already big on providing remote access. Having more distance students just supports that idea!
4. Not really
5. Increased purchase of ebooks and online databases. Also, increased purchase of physical books dealing with online student issues and distance education!
6. We have made a great effort to subscribe to more full-text databases. Also, we have started looking into expanding our ebook collection.
7. I don't think very much. Our library has been moving towards digital resources; the Distance Education students have benefited.
8. We have subscribed to more full-text databases. Ebooks are generally not used and are seldom considered in collection development.
9. Greater emphasis on electronic journals and ebooks in these areas.
10. Yes, influences us to purchase more online.
11. The library has looked to develop access to more e-resources and work closer with local colleges.
12. Very little. Most of the courses developed are distance versions of on-campus courses. For those that are completely new, we do an assessment of the library collection to see if the course can be supported with existing resources; if not, then the department comes up with the dollars to transfer to the library to purchase materials.
13. Distance students are not taken into consideration when developing our collection.
14. Purchase more ebooks.
15. We have tried to increase our offerings of full-text databases, ebooks, and streaming videos.
16. There have not been enough students previously to do this. The only instance I can think of is that we have bought electronic access to electronic journals for single years to meet the needs of one particular cohort.
17. No more than any other course; materials are purchased as required to support the courses (books are posted to students)
18. Not really.
19. Buying more e-resources.
20. So far, not at all. The number of DL students is still fairly low.
21. Very little impact.

22. We ensure that as many online resources as possible are available off-campus. We set up a proxy server for off-campus access. We also purchased far more electronic reference materials to help those who cannot get to the print reference collection.
23. I don't believe that our collection development strategy has changed as a result of our distance students.
24. Increased attention to full-text electronic resources, and some shifting of budgetary priorities.
25. We are incorporating more electronic books into our collections, both reference and traditional monographic materials, in hopes that these might prove useful to many off-site users. We have flipped numerous print journal subscriptions to online only. We promote and encourage awareness and participation in publication of open access journals, courseware, and other types of resources.
26. No, we have a tradition of a strong electronic-resource focus.
27. Our focus is shifting to more digital and electronic resources in place of print.
28. No.
29. We have looked for site licenses of databases, online journals, and are evaluating reference sources for distance use. We also look at database licensing agreements more carefully to look for access for our distance students.
30. Expedited the acquisition of electronic resources.
31. Yes, we tend to collect more materials in electronic format in subjects where we have the most distance learners (e.g., nursing).
32. Even a dozen years ago we tried hard not to get a database unless it was accessible online (at the time that might mean dial-up). Now we won't consider a database that is not accessible online, and that can work through our proxy server. We strongly prefer one with full-text and we expect to be able to tie it into our journal aggregation system and tools. In certain areas we rarely consider a reference book unless it is accessible electronically and we're slowly building up a larger ebook collection. We keep an eye on potential future areas of development while keeping in mind that our distance students tend to be a bit LESS technology-savvy than the traditional college students.
33. Little if any impact.
34. The university does not have a significant distance learning program. The program has not impacted the collection development strategy of the library.
35. Minimally.
36. Insignificantly.
37. We have acquired more electronic resources.
38. If there was no DL, we would not have a library since our library is entirely online. All collection development is predicated on service to both DL and traditional onsite students.
39. We plan to provide electronic reserves and are selecting more electronic resources to benefit traditional and distance learning students.
40. At this point it has not.
41. Affects number of copies of print items for loan; emphasis on electronic resources
42. We buy more online resources to suit both our distance and face to face students; students don't go to the 'shelved' collection much anymore.
43. Ebooks and ejournals are considered necessary sources.
44. I am spending more on Web-based resources of all kinds.
45. We still do about the same collection development, only we choose electronic resources instead of print when we can.
46. We have invested a very major segment of our funds in electronic books and databases (journal articles, reference works, etc).
47. We have added duplicate materials to be made available at distance sites.

48. We subsribe to more electronic resources such as ebooks and databases.
49. We are trying to acquire more electronic resources, especially virtual reference books.
50. Yes, greater emphasis on remote access to research tools and ebooks.
51. We are in general moving toward purchasing more online resources and less in paper. However, this is due to space and general student preferences -- not just the needs on online students. I do purchase a number of online books, particularly for our distance students.
52. Library pays attention to ILL requests. We make selections from this pool of items. Distance education also provides some finaces for library electronic resources that would benefit DL.
53. We purchased a 30,000+ collection of ebooks from ebrary, we are looking at expanding our research databases as well.
54. No difference between distance learning and traditional class materials. The instructors have not presented the need for electronic reserves nor have we pursued this yet.
55. Everyone, on-campus and off-campus, wants more online resources. This has benefited the distance learners.
56. When purchasing books/journals, we attempt to get electronic versions if possible so the distance learning students may easily access them.
57. We have increased our collection of ebooks.
58. Larger purchasing of e-resources.
59. There has been significant positive impact. The library receives funding from Extended Programs, which pays for many of our electronic resources. In my opinion DE was the catalyst that drove us into the electronic era.
60. We have increased the number of Electronic books in our catalog and the subscription databases. For those students who can come to campus, their need for resources should be the same as traditional students -- who we also need to find ways to serve better.
61. We have a budget to do collection development at five public libraries where we have intergovernmental agreements. We have purchased a significant number of online databases and ebook collections. As I embed more and more into classes, and work with the students on their assignments, I get a better sense for which subject areas we are well stocked in and those areas that we need to beef up. We see it as a priority to continually improve our collection development for distance students.
62. Some impact. We choose to provide as many resources online as possible, but that is done with both the distance and campus populations in mind.
63. A work in progress. Not very much, but this could change within the next year.
64. More eBooks are being considered.
65. All collection development is geared for distance learning.
66. Collection development needs of remote access preceded the university's distance learning program.
67. It pushes a digitalization process and usage of electronic resource.
68. Just starting.
69. Not at all, to my knowledge.
70. Yes and no, 24/7 access is important but for all students since we are a "commuter" school.
71. We do not have a single or central DL program, so it is difficult to draw many conclusions. There is more consideration of online access and off-campus access when selecting materials, especially in collections heavily used by DL students, particularly business students.
72. We actively collect books in an electronic format for the fully online Emergency Services Management program, and reference materials that would pertain to the distance ed programs. I also buy books regarding teaching and learning online.

73. Everything we purchase is in digital format. We recently stopped providing print books through our document delivery service and made significant ebook purchases.
74. They go hand in hand and are inseparable, since all our students are, in effect, distance learners (although some students do meet face-to-face sometimes). Obviously, this means we have no physical collection; all our resources and services are based around the online environment.
75. Not at all.
76. Off-campus librarians participate in collection development activities; acquisition of both print and online resources is based on academic programs offered both on and off-campus; collection development policies, while distinct, are based on shared objectives.
77. I don't think distance education plays a role in our collection development.
78. Yes.
79. Conscious effort to acquire full text online, both periodical and monograph.
80. It hasn't that I'm aware of, except for one small microcampus collection where we purchase extra copies of key texts.
81. Our needs are always taken into account in building our database and electronic resources collection.
82. We acquired the BC Open University in 2005, and fully integrated their library in 2007. We are in the process of examining how our collection development strategy meets their needs.
83. It really has affected the use of electronic databases most of all. We have quite a few more now. In addition, the Library purchased all six of the shared collections of NetLibrary.
84. Not at all; no one makes any needs known. That said, most of our distance learning is for students already on campus, so presumably many of them use our services directly as they would for any of their other classes. We have tried to purchase more online materials, but that would be good for all students, not just online students.

Chapter Nine: Sending Books and Periodicals to Distance Learning Students

The mean shipping costs accrued annually by sending physical books, magazines and other educational materials to distance learners was $2,048, with a median of $75 and maximum of $19,850. Non-U.S. institutions reported a mean of over 5 times more than U.S. institutions, $5,381 to $1,096. The lowest mean was for community colleges which spent just over $267 yearly on shipping costs, while four-year degree-granting colleges reported a mean of $6,666. This high mean does include the maximum amount given as $19,850. Research universities also reported a high mean, $5,093, while MA or PhD-granting colleges reported a mean of $1,054. Public colleges spent an average of $2,606, compared to just $781 by private colleges. It should be noted, however, that their medians were much closer, 100 and 50 respectively. Institutions with more than 12,000 FTE students reported a mean of $3,564, while institutions with fewer than 12,000 FTE students reported under $1,950. The lowest amount spent was by institutions with fewer than 2,500 FTE students, which reported spending $1,309 yearly. There was a direct relationship between amount spent annually on shipping costs to send educational materials to distance learners and the number of FTE distance learners. In fact, institutions with over 2,000 FTE distance learners reported a mean of $6,587 and median of $3,250. Institutions with between 1,000 and 2,000 FTE distance learners reported a mean of $2,645 and median of $475. Colleges with between 250 and 999 FTE distance learners reported a mean of $1,383 and median of 50. Those with fewer than 250 FTE distance learning students reported a mean of $221 and median of $50. Institutions whose distance learners living more than 50 miles from campus comprised between 51 and 79% reported a relatively high mean of $7,283 and median of $2,000, whereas institutions whose distance learners living more than 50 miles from campus comprised between 25 and 50% of the distance learners reported a mean of $2,327 and a median of $100.

Over 58% of the sample reported that their usual method of shipping books and other documents to distance learners was through the U.S. Postal Service. Just 1.27% reported that they used certified U.S. mail. Over 24% reported using UPS or another commercial shipper, and over 16% reported using the official state mail service of a country other than the U.S. In fact, over 74% of U.S. respondents reported using U.S. mail with just 1.6% using certified U.S. mail. Just over 76% of non-U.S. respondents reported using their official country's mail service. Just under a quarter of respondents, both U.S. and non-U.S., reported using UPS or another commercial shipper. Just 3.23% of MA or PhD-granting colleges were the only respondents to report using U.S. certified mail. Approximately 75% of all respondents used government mail, with the remainder using commercial shippers, with the exception of four-year degree-granting colleges, only 17% of whom reported using commercial shippers. One-third of these colleges used their non-U.S. government mail, while half used U.S. mail.

Private colleges used commercial shippers significantly more than public colleges did; 20% of public colleges used commercial shippers, compared to 35% of private colleges. Commercial shippers were generally more popular with schools with larger FTE enrollments than those with smaller FTE enrollments. Fully 33% of colleges with over 12,000 FTE students reported using primarily commercial shippers, compared to 28% of institutions with 2,500 to 6,000 FTE students, 21% of institutions with 6,001 to 12,000 FTE students, and 16% of institutions with fewer than 2,500 FTE students. Use of commercial shippers also increased considerably as the number of FTE distance learners decreased. In fact, for institutions with over 1,000 FTE distance learners, no more than 15% of the respondents used commercial shippers as their primary method of shipment. Meanwhile, almost 27% of institutions with between 250 and 999 FTE distance learners and a whopping 42% of institutions with fewer than 250 FTE distance learners reported using UPS or other commercial shippers. The only institutions to report using certified U.S. mail were ones with over 2,000 FTE distance learners. Institutions whose students living more than 50 miles from campus comprised more than 80% or less than 24% of the distance learning students reported the highest percentages of using commercial shipping, 35 and 33%, respectively. Almost 27% of institutions whose distance learning students living more than 50 miles comprised between 51 and 79% of their distance learners and 15% of the institutions whose distance learners living more than 50 miles from campus comprised between 25 an 50% of the distance learners reported using commercial shippers.

The majority of the sample, over 77%, reported that the library's interlibrary loan staff was in responsible for satisfying distance learners' requests for physical copies of books or articles from the library. Another 14% reported that this was the responsibility of the library's distance learning staff, while just over 8% reported that this was part of the job responsibility of another department within the library. Non-U.S. respondents were 3 times more likely thatn U.S. respondents to report that satisfying these requests for physical copies of library materials was the responsibility of the library's distance learning staff. Non-U.S. respondents were also much more likely to report that another department in the library was in charge of such things; over 23% of non-U.S. respondents reported that another library department was in charge of this, compared to just 4.5% of U.S. respondents.

Almost 83% of community colleges and over 78% of MA or PhD-granting colleges reported that the library's interlibrary loan staff was in charge of fulfillment, while four-year degree-granting colleges and research universities both reported that approximately 72% of them had the interlibrary loan staff satisfy the distance learners' needs. Public colleges were almost twice as likely as private colleges to have the library's distance learning staff fulfill requests for physical library materials, making private colleges (82%) more likely than public colleges (76%) to use the interlibrary loan staff to satisfy such requests.

Institutions with mid-sized FTE enrollments, between 2,500 and 12,000, reported relatively high percentages having some other library department fulfilling these requests, over 10%. Just 5% of institutions with more than 12,000 or fewer than 2,500 students reported the same. Three in 10 colleges with over 12,000 FTE students, however, reported that the library's distance learning staff was in charge of these fulfillments, compared to just 15% of institutions with between 2,500 and 6,000 FTE students, 8% of institutions with between 6,001 and 12,000 FTE students, and just 5% of those with fewer than 2,500 FTE students. Colleges with the highest number of FTE distance learners, over 2,000, reported that 37.5% of them had the library's distance learning staff handle these requests, 62.5% had their interlibrary loan staff handle them, and none reported using another department. Colleges with fewer FTE distance learners were more likely to use the library's interlibrary loan staff to handle distance learning students' requests for physical materials from the library. Almost 7% of colleges with between 1,000 and 2,000 FTE distance learners used the distance learning staff at the library to fulfill requests, and over 13% reported that another library department handled them. No institution with between 250 and 999 FTE distance learners reported using the distance learning staff that library, and 6.7% reported using another department. An even 15% of institutions with fewer than 250 FTE distance learners used the library's distance learning staff for such fulfillment, and another 10% reported used some other department within the library. The higher the proportion of distance learners that live more than 50 miles from campus, the more likely fulfillment is handled by the library's distance learning staff. 30% of institutions whose distance learners living more than 50 miles from campus comprised more than 80% of their distance learners reported this, compared to 18.75% of institutions in the next tier, whose distance learners living more than 50 miles away comprised 51 to 79% of the distance learners, 5% of institutions whose distance learners living more than 50 miles away comprised between 25 and 50% of the distance learners, and none of the institutions whose distance learners living more than 50 miles away comprised less than 24% of the distance learning students. In fact, institutions whose distance learners living so far away comprised less than 24% of the total distance learners reported that 100% of such requests are fulfilled by interlibrary loan staff. Six to 10% of institutions with higher proportions of distance learners living more than 50 miles away reported using another library department to fulfill these requests.

Just over half of the sample, over 52%, had no restrictions on the delivery of books, articles and other paper versions of intellectual property to distance learners, meaning that they deliver such materials even if the students live close to campus. Almost 36% delivered materials only if reciepients live a certain distance from campus, while 11% delivered books only to satellite sites from which students pick up the books. There was little difference between the U.S. and non-U.S. participants, except that U.S. libraries were twice as likely as non-U.S. libraries to send materials only to satellite sites for students to pick up.

Community colleges were slightly more likely to restrict where they might send library materials; only half will send materials to students no matter where they live. MA or PhD-granting colleges were next at almost 52%, while over 57% of both four-year degree-granting colleges and research universities do not put restrictions on sending materials. Almost 32% of community colleges and 33% of research universities reported only sending materials if the distance learning students lived a specified distance away from campus, while almost 39% of MA or PhD granting colleges and nearly 43% of four-year degree granting colleges reported the same. No four-year degree-granting college reported that they only send books to satellite sites, while 18.2% of community colleges use this system. By comparison, almost 10% of MA or PhD granting colleges and research universities send materials only to satellite sites. There was little difference between public and private colleges' restrictions on sending library materials to distance learning students, but public colleges were slightly more likely to not put restrictions on sending materials, and less likely to send materials exclusively to satellite sites for students to pick up.

Colleges with over 6,001 FTE students were more likely to only deliver books to distance learners living a certain distance away from campus. Four of 10 colleges with over 12,000 FTE students and five out of 10 colleges with between 6,001 and 12,000 FTE students restrict delivery of library materials in this way, compared to just 21% of colleges with between 2,500 and 6,000 FTE students and 28% of colleges with fewer than 2,500 FTE students.

Over 21% of institutions with between 2,500 and 6,000 FTE students, the highest percentage reported, use the satellite system and only send books to sites where students can pick up the materials. Two in three colleges with between 1,000 and 2,000 FTE distance learners reported not restricting the delivery of library materials, while 53% of institutions with over 2,000 FTE distance learners, 40% of institutions with between 250 and 999 distance learners, and 50% of institutions with under 250 distance learners reported the same.

As the number of FTE distance learners decreased, the use of the satellite system increased: 6.67% in institutions with over 1,000 FTE distance learners and 15% in institutions with fewer than 250 FTE distance learners.

The vast majority of the sample, close to 89%, reported that the cost of shipping library materials to distance learners was generally paid for by the library. Over 7% reported that the costs are covered by the student, while close to 4% reported that costs are covered by the student through a special fee, regardless of the number of items shipped. This last option was popular with close to 6% of non-U.S. respondents, while chosen by only 3% of U.S. participants. For U.S. participants, costs are more often paid for by the student (7.8%) than with non-U.S. participants (5.9%). Libraries in each Carnegie class reported that between 86 and 93% of them had the library pay for shipping library materials, except for four-year degree granting colleges, only 71% of whom reported paying for it through the library. Instead, 14.3% of them reported that the student paid for shipping fees, and another 14.3% reported that it was a special flat fee paid by the student, regardless of the number of items shipped. Private colleges were over 6 times more likely than public colleges to use this flat fee paid by the student system, and also more likely to have the student pay the full amount of the shipping fees.

Institutions used the flat fee paid by the student more often as the number of FTE students at the institution decreased; no institution with over 12,000 FTE students used this practice, while 5.26% of institutions with fewer than 6,000 FTE students did. Colleges with higher enrollments generally had the library pay for such shipping fees. The same is not true of institutions with increasingly large FTE distance learners, however; colleges with over 2,000 or under FTE distance learners reported that just 82-83% of them had the library cover shipping costs, while 100% of institutions with between 250 and 2,000 FTE distance learners reported that such costs were covered by the library. Instead, 5.9% of institutions with the most distance learners reported that the student bore the costs per piece and 11.8% said students paid through a special flat fee. Institutions with the smallest number of FTE distance learners were more likely to have the student cover the full cost (11%) and less likely to charge the flat fee (5.6%).

No institution with fewer than 24% of their distance learners living more than 50 miles from campus had the students cover the costs of shipping. However, almost 95% of institutions with more than 80% of their distance learners living more than 50 miles away also reported that the library covered such costs, with the remainder, 5.3%, reporting that the costs are covered by the student.

Just eight in 10 institutions with between 25 and 79% of their distance learners living more than 50 miles away reported that the library covered the shipping costs, with the remainder being covered by the student through full or flat fees.

Table 9.1: Mean, Median, Minimum and Maximum Estimated Shipping Costs Accrued Annually by Sending Physical Books, Magazines or Other Educational Materials to Distance Learners, in US$

	Mean	Median	Minimum	Maximum
Entire Sample	2,048.28	75.00	0.00	19,850.00

Table 9.2: Mean, Median, Minimum and Maximum Estimated Shipping Costs Accrued Annually by Sending Physical Books, Magazines or Other Educational Materials to Distance Learners, in US$, Broken Out by U.S. and Non-U.S. Libraries

U.S. and Non-U.S. Libraries	Mean	Median	Minimum	Maximum
U.S.	1,096.00	50.00	0.00	8,000.00
Non-U.S.	5,381.25	1,550.00	0.00	19,850.00

Table 9.3: Mean, Median, Minimum and Maximum Estimated Shipping Costs Accrued Annually by Sending Physical Books, Magazines or Other Educational Materials to Distance Learners, in US$, Broken Out by Carnegie Class

Carnegie Class	Mean	Median	Minimum	Maximum
Community College	267.65	0.00	0.00	2,000.00
4-Year Degree Granting College	6,666.67	100.00	50.00	19,850.00
MA or PhD Granting College	1,054.88	150.00	0.00	4,500.00
Research University	5,093.63	4,774.50	100.00	10,000.00

Table 9.4: Mean, Median, Minimum and Maximum Estimated Shipping Costs Accrued Annually by Sending Physical Books, Magazines or Other Educational Materials to Distance Learners, in US$, Broken Out by Public or Private Status

Public or Private Status	Mean	Median	Minimum	Maximum
Public College	2,605.96	100.00	0.00	19,850.00
Private College	780.82	50.00	0.00	4,500.00

Table 9.5: **Mean, Median, Minimum and Maximum Estimated Shipping Costs Accrued Annually by Sending Physical Books, Magazines or Other Educational Materials to Distance Learners, in US$, Broken Out by Number of FTE Students at the Institution**

Number of FTE Students at the Institution	Mean	Median	Minimum	Maximum
>12,000	3,564.29	50.00	0.00	19,850.00
6,001-12,000	1,850.00	300.00	0.00	10,000.00
2,500-6,000	1,948.91	0.00	0.00	10,000.00
<2,500	1,309.09	100.00	0.00	8,000.00

Table 9.6: **Mean, Median, Minimum and Maximum Estimated Shipping Costs Accrued Annually by Sending Physical Books, Magazines or Other Educational Materials to Distance Learners, in US$, Broken Out by Number of FTE Distance Learners**

Number of FTE Distance Learners	Mean	Median	Minimum	Maximum
>2,000	6,587.50	3,250.00	0.00	19,850.00
1,000-2,000	2,645.00	475.00	0.00	10,000.00
250-999	1,383.33	50.00	0.00	10,000.00
<250	221.43	50.00	0.00	1,250.00

Table 9.7: **Mean, Median, Minimum and Maximum Estimated Shipping Costs Accrued Annually by Sending Physical Books, Magazines or Other Educational Materials to Distance Learners, in US$, Broken Out by Percentage of Distance Learners Living More than 50 Miles from Campus**

Percentage of Distance Learners Living More than 50 Miles from Campus	Mean	Median	Minimum	Maximum
80-100%	2,168.75	675.00	0.00	8,000.00
51-79%	7,283.33	2,000.00	0.00	19,850.00
25-50%	2,327.18	100.00	0.00	10,000.00
1-24%	848.90	25.00	0.00	4,500.00

Table 9.8:   The Library's Primary Method of Shipment of Books and Other Documents to Distance Learners

	US Mail	US Mail, Certified	UPS or other commercial shipper	Official state mail service of country other than the USA
Entire Sample	58.23%	1.27%	24.05%	16.46%

Table 9.9:   The Library's Primary Method of Shipment of Books and Other Documents to Distance Learners, Broken Out by U.S. and Non-U.S. Libraries

U.S. and Non-U.S. Libraries	US Mail	US Mail, Certified	UPS or other commercial shipper	Official state mail service of country other than the USA
U.S.	74.19%	1.61%	24.19%	0.00%
Non-U.S.	0.00%	0.00%	23.53%	76.47%

Table 9.10:   The Library's Primary Method of Shipment of Books and Other Documents to Distance Learners, Broken Out by Carnegie Class

Carnegie Class	US Mail	US Mail, Certified	UPS or other commercial shipper	Official state mail service of country other than the USA
Community College	68.18%	0.00%	22.73%	9.09%
4-Year Degree Granting College	50.00%	0.00%	16.67%	33.33%
MA or PhD Granting College	61.29%	3.23%	25.81%	9.68%
Research University	45.00%	0.00%	25.00%	30.00%

Table 9.11:   The Library's Primary Method of Shipment of Books and Other Documents to Distance Learners, Broken Out by Public or Private Status

Public or Private Status	US Mail	US Mail, Certified	UPS or other commercial shipper	Official state mail service of country other than the USA
Public College	57.63%	1.69%	20.34%	20.34%
Private College	60.00%	0.00%	35.00%	5.00%

Table 9.12: The Library's Primary Method of Shipment of Books and Other Documents to Distance Learners, Broken Out by Number of FTE Students at the Institution

Number of FTE Students at the Institution	US Mail	US Mail, Certified	UPS or other commercial shipper	Official state mail service of country other than the USA
>12,000	33.33%	0.00%	33.33%	33.33%
6,001-12,000	62.50%	0.00%	20.83%	16.67%
2,500-6,000	55.56%	5.56%	27.78%	11.11%
<2,500	78.95%	0.00%	15.79%	5.26%

Table 9.13: The Library's Primary Method of Shipment of Books and Other Documents to Distance Learners, Broken Out by Number of FTE Distance Learners

Number of FTE Distance Learners	US Mail	US Mail, Certified	UPS or other commercial shipper	Official state mail service of country other than the USA
>2,000	61.54%	7.69%	15.38%	15.38%
1,000-2,000	60.00%	0.00%	13.33%	26.67%
250-999	66.67%	0.00%	26.67%	6.67%
<250	47.37%	0.00%	42.11%	10.53%

Table 9.14: The Library's Primary Method of Shipment of Books and Other Documents to Distance Learners, Broken Out by Percentage of Distance Learners Living More than 50 Miles from Campus

Percentage of Distance Learners Living More than 50 Miles from Campus	US Mail	US Mail, Certified	UPS or other commercial shipper	Official state mail service of country other than the USA
80-100%	40.00%	0.00%	35.00%	25.00%
51-79%	46.67%	0.00%	26.67%	26.67%
25-50%	65.00%	5.00%	15.00%	15.00%
1-24%	66.67%	0.00%	33.33%	0.00%

Table 9.15: Library Staff Responsible for Satisfying Distance Learners' Requests for Physical Copies of Books or Articles from the Library

	The Library's Distance Learning Staff	The Library's Interlibrary Loan Staff	Another Department of the Library
Entire Sample	14.29%	77.38%	8.33%

**Table 9.16: Library Staff Responsible for Satisfying Distance Learners'
Requests for Physical Copies of Books or Articles from the Library, Broken Out by
U.S. and Non-U.S. Libraries**

U.S. and Non-U.S. Libraries	The Library's Distance Learning Staff	The Library's Interlibrary Loan Staff	Another Department of the Library
U.S.	10.45%	85.07%	4.48%
Non-U.S.	29.41%	47.06%	23.53%

**Table 9.17: Library Staff Responsible for Satisfying Distance Learners'
Requests for Physical Copies of Books or Articles from the Library, Broken Out by
Carnegie Class**

Carnegie Class	The Library's Distance Learning Staff	The Library's Interlibrary Loan Staff	Another Department of the Library
Community College	4.35%	82.61%	13.04%
4-Year Degree Granting College	14.29%	71.43%	14.29%
MA or PhD Granting College	18.75%	78.13%	3.13%
Research University	18.18%	72.73%	9.09%

**Table 9.18: Library Staff Responsible for Satisfying Distance Learners'
Requests for Physical Copies of Books or Articles from the Library, Broken Out by
Public or Private Status**

Public or Private Status	The Library's Distance Learning Staff	The Library's Interlibrary Loan Staff	Another Department of the Library
Public College	16.13%	75.81%	8.06%
Private College	9.09%	81.82%	9.09%

**Table 9.19: Library Staff Responsible for Satisfying Distance Learners'
Requests for Physical Copies of Books or Articles from the Library, Broken Out by
Number of FTE Students at the Institution**

Number of FTE Students at the Institution	The Library's Distance Learning Staff	The Library's Interlibrary Loan Staff	Another Department of the Library
>12,000	30.00%	65.00%	5.00%
6,001-12,000	8.33%	79.17%	12.50%
2,500-6,000	15.00%	75.00%	10.00%
<2,500	5.00%	90.00%	5.00%

Table 9.20:   Library Staff Responsible for Satisfying Distance Learners' Requests for Physical Copies of Books or Articles from the Library, Broken Out by Number of FTE Distance Learners

Number of FTE Distance Learners	The Library's Distance Learning Staff	The Library's Interlibrary Loan Staff	Another Department of the Library
>2,000	37.50%	62.50%	0.00%
1,000-2,000	6.67%	80.00%	13.33%
250-999	0.00%	93.33%	6.67%
<250	15.00%	75.00%	10.00%

Table 9.21:   Library Staff Responsible for Satisfying Distance Learners' Requests for Physical Copies of Books or Articles from the Library, Broken Out by Percentage of Distance Learners Living More than 50 Miles from Campus

Percentage of Distance Learners Living More than 50 Miles from Campus	The Library's Distance Learning Staff	The Library's Interlibrary Loan Staff	Another Department of the Library
80-100%	30.00%	60.00%	10.00%
51-79%	18.75%	75.00%	6.25%
25-50%	5.00%	85.00%	10.00%
1-24%	0.00%	100.00%	0.00%

Table 9.22:   Restrictions on the Delivery of Books, Articles and Other Paper Versions of Intellectual Property to Distance Learners

	Wherever they live even if they live close to campus	Only if they live a certain specified distance from campus	Only to satellite sites from which they can pick up the books
Entire Sample	53.09%	35.80%	11.11%

Table 9.23:   Restrictions on the Delivery of Books, Articles and Other Paper Versions of Intellectual Property to Distance Learners, Broken Out by U.S. and Non-U.S. Libraries

U.S. and Non-U.S. Libraries	Wherever they live even if they live close to campus	Only if they live a certain specified distance from campus	Only to satellite sites from which they can pick up the books
U.S.	52.38%	34.92%	12.70%
Non-U.S.	55.56%	38.89%	5.56%

Table 9.24:   Restrictions on the Delivery of Books, Articles and Other Paper Versions of Intellectual Property to Distance Learners, Broken Out by Carnegie Class

Carnegie Class	Wherever they live even if they live close to campus	Only if they live a certain specified distance from campus	Only to satellite sites from which they can pick up the books
Community College	50.00%	31.82%	18.18%
4-Year Degree Granting College	57.14%	42.86%	0.00%
MA or PhD Granting College	51.61%	38.71%	9.68%
Research University	57.14%	33.33%	9.52%

Table 9.25:   Restrictions on the Delivery of Books, Articles and Other Paper Versions of Intellectual Property to Distance Learners, Broken Out by Public or Private Status

Public or Private Status	Wherever they live even if they live close to campus	Only if they live a certain specified distance from campus	Only to satellite sites from which they can pick up the books
Public College	54.10%	36.07%	9.84%
Private College	50.00%	35.00%	15.00%

Table 9.26:   Restrictions on the Delivery of Books, Articles and Other Paper Versions of Intellectual Property to Distance Learners, Broken Out by Number of FTE Students at the Institution

Number of FTE Students at the Institution	Wherever they live even if they live close to campus	Only if they live a certain specified distance from campus	Only to satellite sites from which they can pick up the books
>12,000	55.00%	40.00%	5.00%
6,001-12,000	41.67%	50.00%	8.33%
2,500-6,000	57.89%	21.05%	21.05%
<2,500	61.11%	27.78%	11.11%

Table 9.27:   Restrictions on the Delivery of Books, Articles and Other Paper Versions of Intellectual Property to Distance Learners, Broken Out by Number of FTE Distance Learners

Number of FTE Distance Learners	Wherever they live even if they live close to campus	Only if they live a certain specified distance from campus	Only to satellite sites from which they can pick up the books
>2,000	53.33%	40.00%	6.67%
1,000-2,000	66.67%	26.67%	6.67%
250-999	40.00%	46.67%	13.33%
<250	50.00%	35.00%	15.00%

Table 9.28:   Restrictions on the Delivery of Books, Articles and Other Paper Versions of Intellectual Property to Distance Learners, Broken Out by Percentage of Distance Learners Living More than 50 Miles from Campus

Percentage of Distance Learners Living More than 50 Miles from Campus	Wherever they live even if they live close to campus	Only if they live a certain specified distance from campus	Only to satellite sites from which they can pick up the books
80-100%	55.00%	40.00%	5.00%
51-79%	43.75%	50.00%	6.25%
25-50%	63.16%	26.32%	10.53%
1-24%	37.50%	43.75%	18.75%

Table 9.29:   Entity that Covers the Cost of Shipping Library Books and Periodicals to Distance Learners

	Generally paid by the library	Generally paid by the student	Paid by the student through a special fee regardless of the number of items shipped
Entire Sample	88.89%	7.41%	3.70%

Table 9.30:   Entity that Covers the Cost of Shipping Library Books and Periodicals to Distance Learners, Broken Out by U.S. and Non-U.S. Libraries

U.S. and Non-U.S. Libraries	Generally paid by the library	Generally paid by the student	Paid by the student through a special fee regardless of the number of items shipped
U.S.	89.06%	7.81%	3.13%
Non-U.S.	88.24%	5.88%	5.88%

Table 9.31:   Entity that Covers the Cost of Shipping Library Books and Periodicals to Distance Learners, Broken Out by Carnegie Class

Carnegie Class	Generally paid by the library	Generally paid by the student	Paid by the student through a special fee regardless of the number of items shipped
Community College	91.30%	8.70%	0.00%
4-Year Degree Granting College	71.43%	14.29%	14.29%
MA or PhD Granting College	93.33%	3.33%	3.33%
Research University	85.71%	9.52%	4.76%

Table 9.32:   Entity that Covers the Cost of Shipping Library Books and Periodicals to Distance Learners, Broken Out by Public or Private Status

Public or Private Status	Generally paid by the library	Generally paid by the student	Paid by the student through a special fee regardless of the number of items shipped
Public College	91.80%	6.56%	1.64%
Private College	80.00%	10.00%	10.00%

Table 9.33:   Entity that Covers the Cost of Shipping Library Books and Periodicals to Distance Learners, Broken Out by Number of FTE Students at the Institution

Number of FTE Students at the Institution	Generally paid by the library	Generally paid by the student	Paid by the student through a special fee regardless of the number of items shipped
>12,000	94.74%	5.26%	0.00%
6,001-12,000	83.33%	12.50%	4.17%
2,500-6,000	89.47%	5.26%	5.26%
<2,500	89.47%	5.26%	5.26%

Table 9.34:   Entity that Covers the Cost of Shipping Library Books and Periodicals to Distance Learners, Broken Out by Number of FTE Distance Learners

Number of FTE Distance Learners	Generally paid by the library	Generally paid by the student	Paid by the student through a special fee regardless of the number of items shipped
>2,000	82.35%	5.88%	11.76%
1,000-2,000	100.00%	0.00%	0.00%
250-999	100.00%	0.00%	0.00%
<250	83.33%	11.11%	5.56%

Table 9.35: Entity that Covers the Cost of Shipping Library Books and Periodicals to Distance Learners, Broken Out by Percentage of Distance Learners Living More than 50 Miles from Campus

Percentage of Distance Learners Living More than 50 Miles from Campus	Generally paid by the library	Generally paid by the student	Paid by the student through a special fee regardless of the number of items shipped
80-100%	94.74%	5.26%	0.00%
51-79%	82.35%	11.76%	5.88%
25-50%	80.00%	10.00%	10.00%
1-24%	100.00%	0.00%	0.00%

Chapter Ten: Courseware

Barely 39% of participants in the sample provide remote assistance to students in the use of their courseware packages, such as WebCT, Blackboard, and others. Over 40% of U.S. institutions offered this assistance, compared to just under 32% of non-U.S. respondents. Over 54% of research universities and nearly 43% of four-year degree-granting colleges offered this assistance, while just 35% of community colleges and 31% of MA or PhD-granting colleges did. Nearly 44% of public colleges provided remote assistance, while just 24% of private colleges did.

There was no direct relationship between the number of FTE students at the institution and whether remote assistance was available for courseware, and there was little variation across the various tiers of enrollment size. There was a strong correlation between this type of remote help and the number of FTE distance learners. Half of all colleges with over 2,000 FTE distance learners offered this help, compared with 42% of institutions with between 1,000 and 2,000 FTE distance learners, 30% of those with between 250 and 999 FTE distance learners, and 28.6% of those with fewer than 250 FTE distance learners.

There was no strong correlation between the proportion of distance learners living more than 50 miles from campus and the availability of remote assistance for courseware, but institutions with the highest (over 80%) and lowest (below 24%) percentage of distance learners living more than 50 miles from campus reported similar numbers; 35% had such help available to students.

Table 10.1:   Libraries that Provide Remote Assistance to Students in the Use of their Courseware Packages such as WebCT, Blackboard and Others

	Yes	No
Entire Sample	38.78%	61.22%

Table 10.2:   Libraries that Provide Remote Assistance to Students in the Use of their Courseware Packages such as WebCT, Blackboard and Others, Broken Out by U.S. and Non-U.S. Libraries

U.S. and Non-U.S. Libraries	Yes	No
U.S.	40.51%	59.49%
Non-U.S.	31.58%	68.42%

Table 10.3:   Libraries that Provide Remote Assistance to Students in the Use of their Courseware Packages such as WebCT, Blackboard and Others, Broken Out by Carnegie Class

Carnegie Class	Yes	No
Community College	35.29%	64.71%
4-Year Degree Granting College	42.86%	57.14%
MA or PhD Granting College	31.43%	68.57%
Research University	54.55%	45.45%

Table 10.4: **Libraries that Provide Remote Assistance to Students in the Use of their Courseware Packages such as WebCT, Blackboard and Others, Broken Out by Public or Private Status**

Public or Private Status	Yes	No
Public College	43.84%	56.16%
Private College	24.00%	76.00%

Table 10.5: **Libraries that Provide Remote Assistance to Students in the Use of their Courseware Packages such as WebCT, Blackboard and Others, Broken Out by Number of FTE Students at the Institution**

Number of FTE Students at the Institution	Yes	No
>12,000	41.67%	58.33%
6,001-12,000	36.00%	64.00%
2,500-6,000	40.00%	60.00%
<2,500	37.50%	62.50%

Table 10.6: **Libraries that Provide Remote Assistance to Students in the Use of their Courseware Packages such as WebCT, Blackboard and Others, Broken Out by Number of FTE Distance Learners**

Number of FTE Distance Learners	Yes	No
>2,000	50.00%	50.00%
1,000-2,000	42.11%	57.89%
250-999	30.00%	70.00%
<250	28.57%	71.43%

Table 10.7: **Libraries that Provide Remote Assistance to Students in the Use of their Courseware Packages such as WebCT, Blackboard and Others, Broken Out by Percentage of Distance Learners Living More than 50 Miles from Campus**

Percentage of Distance Learners Living More than 50 Miles from Campus	Yes	No
80-100%	34.78%	65.22%
51-79%	41.18%	58.82%
25-50%	30.43%	69.57%
1-24%	35.00%	65.00%

Chapter Eleven: Copyright and Access Issues

Only a small minority, 3%, reported that more than a quarter of the library databases were inaccessible to distance learners. A third of respondents offered over 75% of their library's databases for remote access, while the majority indicated that all of their library databases were remotely accessible. Over 68% of U.S. institutions reported that their distance learners had full access to the databases remotely, compared to just 42% of non-U.S. libraries. All community colleges and four-year degree-granting colleges in the survey reported offering at least 75% of their library databases remotely, while 5.7% of MA or PhD-granting colleges and 4.6% of research universities failed to do so.

The largest and smallest institutions by FTE enrollment reported the highest percentages of offering full database access to distance learners, compared to schools with just mid-sized enrollments. No institution with more than 6,000 FTE students reported that many of their databases could not be accessed from off campus, while 8% of institutions with fewer than 6,000 FTE students did not offer more than 75% of their databases to distance learners remotely.

Institutions were generally more likely to offer full remote access to their databases as the number of FTE distance learners increased. Colleges with the highest (over 80%) and lowest (under 24%) percentage of their distance learners living more than 50 miles from campus reported the highest percentages, 56.5 and 70%, respectively, offering full remote access to distance learners. Just 47% of institutions with between 51 and 79% of their distance learners living more than 50 miles from campus reported that all of their databases were accessible remotely, but the remainder, almost 53%, reported that at least 75% of their databases were accessible remotely. Over 56% of institutions with between 25 and 50% of their distance learners living more than 50 miles from campus offered full remote access to their databases.

Just 3% of the sample reported that copyright issues relating to access, faxing and photocopying issues for distance learners was a frequent problem. The rest were split evenly, either indicating it was no problem at all or a problem only sometimes. Only non-U.S. participants had frequent problems, with as many as 15.8% indicating as such. Community colleges reported the fewest problems; 76% indicated that copyright issues were never a problem. Almost 43% of four-year degree-granting colleges, 38% of MA or PhD-granting colleges, and 27% of research universities also said that it was not an issue for them. No community college or MA or PhD-granting college reported that copyright issues were a frequent problem. Meanwhile, 14% of four-year degree granting colleges and 9% of research universities reported that copyright issues presented frequent problems.

No private college reported that copyright issues were a frequent problem. Over 62% of colleges with fewer than 2,500 FTE students reported that copyright issues for distance learners was not a problem, while 48% and 41% of colleges in the higher enrollment brackets reported the same. The only colleges that indicated copyright issues were frequently a problem for them were those with over 12,000 FTE students (4.55%) and those between 2,500 and 6,000 FTE students (8%).

Institutions were also less likely to consider copyright issues of access, faxing and photocopying for distance learners a problem at all as the number of FTE distance learners decreased. 22% of colleges with over 2,000 FTE distance learners reported that it was not a problem at all, compared with 67% of institutions with fewer than 250 FTE distance learners. Similarly, participants were more likely to indicate that copyright issues were sometimes a problem as the number of FTE distance learners increased.

For libraries with a budget for copyright materials largely for use by distance learners, mean spending was $15,578. Unfortunately, we did not receive enough data for this question to break out the data according to various criteria.

Table 11.1: Access to the Library's Databases by Distance Learners vs. On-Campus Students

	All of our databases can be accessed remotely	At least 75% of our databases can be accessed remotely	Many of our databases cannot be accessed off campus
Entire Sample	63.27%	33.67%	3.06%

Table 11.2: Access to the Library's Databases by Distance Learners vs. On-Campus Students, Broken Out by U.S. and Non-U.S. Libraries

U.S. and Non-U.S. Libraries	All of our databases can be accessed remotely	At least 75% of our databases can be accessed remotely	Many of our databases cannot be accessed off campus
U.S.	68.35%	29.11%	2.53%
Non-U.S.	42.11%	52.63%	5.26%

Table 11.3: Access to the Library's Databases by Distance Learners vs. On-Campus Students, Broken Out by Carnegie Class

Carnegie Class	All of our databases can be accessed remotely	At least 75% of our databases can be accessed remotely	Many of our databases cannot be accessed off campus
Community College	64.71%	35.29%	0.00%
4-Year Degree Granting College	57.14%	42.86%	0.00%
MA or PhD Granting College	65.71%	28.57%	5.71%
Research University	59.09%	36.36%	4.55%

Table 11.4:   Access to the Library's Databases by Distance Learners vs. On-Campus Students, Broken Out by Public or Private Status

Public or Private Status	All of our databases can be accessed remotely	At least 75% of our databases can be accessed remotely	Many of our databases cannot be accessed off campus
Public College	63.01%	34.25%	2.74%
Private College	64.00%	32.00%	4.00%

Table 11.5:   Access to the Library's Databases by Distance Learners vs. On-Campus Students, Broken Out by Number of FTE Students at the Institution

Number of FTE Students at the Institution	All of our databases can be accessed remotely	At least 75% of our databases can be accessed remotely	Many of our databases cannot be accessed off campus
>12,000	66.67%	33.33%	0.00%
6,001-12,000	60.00%	40.00%	0.00%
2,500-6,000	56.00%	36.00%	8.00%
<2,500	70.83%	25.00%	4.17%

Table 11.6:   Access to the Library's Databases by Distance Learners vs. On-Campus Students, Broken Out by Number of FTE Distance Learners

Number of FTE Distance Learners	All of our databases can be accessed remotely	At least 75% of our databases can be accessed remotely	Many of our databases cannot be accessed off campus
>2,000	66.67%	33.33%	0.00%
1,000-2,000	63.16%	36.84%	0.00%
250-999	60.00%	35.00%	5.00%
<250	61.90%	28.57%	9.52%

Table 11.7:   Access to the Library's Databases by Distance Learners vs. On-Campus Students, Broken Out by Percentage of Distance Learners Living More than 50 Miles from Campus

Percentage of Distance Learners Living More than 50 Miles from Campus	All of our databases can be accessed remotely	At least 75% of our databases can be accessed remotely	Many of our databases cannot be accessed off campus
80-100%	69.57%	26.09%	4.35%
51-79%	47.06%	52.94%	0.00%
25-50%	56.52%	39.13%	4.35%
1-24%	70.00%	25.00%	5.00%

Table 11.8:   Extent to which Copyright Issues Relating to Access, Faxing and Photocopying for Distance Learners are a Problem

	Not a problem at all for us	Sometimes a problem for us	Frequently a problem for us
Entire Sample	48.96%	47.92%	3.13%

Table 11.9:   Extent to which Copyright Issues Relating to Access, Faxing and Photocopying for Distance Learners are a Problem, Broken Out by U.S. and Non-U.S. Libraries

U.S. and Non-U.S. Libraries	Not a problem at all for us	Sometimes a problem for us	Frequently a problem for us
U.S.	49.35%	50.65%	0.00%
Non-U.S.	47.37%	36.84%	15.79%

Table 11.10:   Extent to which Copyright Issues Relating to Access, Faxing and Photocopying for Distance Learners are a Problem, Broken Out by Carnegie Class

Carnegie Class	Not a problem at all for us	Sometimes a problem for us	Frequently a problem for us
Community College	75.76%	24.24%	0.00%
4-Year Degree Granting College	42.86%	42.86%	14.29%
MA or PhD Granting College	38.24%	61.76%	0.00%
Research University	27.27%	63.64%	9.09%

Table 11.11:   Extent to which Copyright Issues Relating to Access, Faxing and Photocopying for Distance Learners are a Problem, Broken Out by Public or Private Status

Public or Private Status	Not a problem at all for us	Sometimes a problem for us	Frequently a problem for us
Public College	50.70%	45.07%	4.23%
Private College	44.00%	56.00%	0.00%

Table 11.12:   Extent to which Copyright Issues Relating to Access, Faxing and Photocopying for Distance Learners are a Problem, Broken Out by Number of FTE Students at the Institution

Number of FTE Students at the Institution	Not a problem at all for us	Sometimes a problem for us	Frequently a problem for us
>12,000	40.91%	54.55%	4.55%
6,001-12,000	48.00%	52.00%	0.00%
2,500-6,000	44.00%	48.00%	8.00%
<2,500	62.50%	37.50%	0.00%

Table 11.13:   Extent to which Copyright Issues Relating to Access, Faxing and Photocopying for Distance Learners are a Problem, Broken Out by Number of FTE Distance Learners

Number of FTE Distance Learners	Not a problem at all for us	Sometimes a problem for us	Frequently a problem for us
>2,000	22.22%	72.22%	5.56%
1,000-2,000	42.11%	52.63%	5.26%
250-999	55.56%	38.89%	5.56%
<250	66.67%	33.33%	0.00%

Table 11.14:   Extent to which Copyright Issues Relating to Access, Faxing and Photocopying for Distance Learner are a Problem, Broken Out by Percentage of Distance Learners Living More than 50 Miles from Campus

Percentage of Distance Learners Living More than 50 Miles from Campus	Not a problem at all for us	Sometimes a problem for us	Frequently a problem for us
80-100%	30.43%	65.22%	4.35%
51-79%	58.82%	35.29%	5.88%
25-50%	59.09%	36.36%	4.55%
1-24%	52.63%	47.37%	0.00%

Table 11.15:   Mean, Median, Minimum and Maximum Amount Spent Annually by Libraries that have a Formal or Informal Budget for Copyright Materials for Databases, Ebooks and Other Copyright Materials that will be Used Largely by Distance Learners, in US$

	Mean	Median	Minimum	Maximum
Entire Sample	15,757.86	8,000.00	0.00	54,505.00

We asked for, but did not receive, enough data to break out the above data.

Chapter Twelve: Professional Standing

Among the libraries that employed distance learning librarianship staff, the mean number of FTE positions allotted was 1.21, with a median of 1. Four-year degree granting colleges reported the highest mean, 2.25, research universities next with 1.27, and other colleges with just 1. Institutions with over 6,001 FTE students reported means of 1.45 to 1.47, while colleges with between 2,500 to 6,000 FTE students reported a mean of .86, and institutions with fewer than 2,500 FTE students reported a mean of .94.

We asked for the annual salary ranges of librarians dedicated largely to distance learners, or the head of distance learning librarianship division, if one existed. Among those survey respondents who indicated having such a position, a third reported this salary range to be between $40,000 and $50,000, with another 28% offering salaries between $50,000 and $65,000. Just 15% reported paying less than $40,000, and just over 4% paid over $85,000.

The bulk of non-U.S. participants offered higher salaries than their U.S. counterparts, but only U.S. participants (5.7%) reported offering salaries above $85,000. While four-year degree granting colleges and research universities offered both low to moderately high salaries, community colleges offered a smaller range but higher up on the pay scale. They were most likely to offer higher salaries, and none reported offering less than $40,000. Private colleges mostly offered salaries in the $40,000 to $50,000 range, while public colleges were more evenly distributed among low and high salary ranges. The pay scale increased as the number of FTE distance learners increased. For colleges with the most FTE distance learners, a whopping 44% reported paying between $65,000 and $85,000. Curiously, though, the only colleges offering salaries of over $85,000 were the ones with fewer than 999 FTE distance learners.

Table 12.1:   Mean, Median, Minimum and Maximum Number of FTE Positions Allotted to Distance Learning Librarianship Among Libraries with Distance Learning Librarianship Staff

	Mean	Median	Minimum	Maximum
Entire Sample	1.21	1.00	0.10	6.00

Table 12.2:   Mean, Median, Minimum and Maximum Number of FTE Positions Allotted to Distance Learning Librarianship Among Libraries with Distance Learning Librarianship Staff, Broken Out by U.S. and Non-U.S. Libraries

U.S. and Non-U.S. Libraries	Mean	Median	Minimum	Maximum
U.S.	1.18	1.00	0.10	6.00
Non-U.S.	1.34	1.00	0.25	2.50

Table 12.3: Mean, Median, Minimum and Maximum Number of FTE Positions Allotted to Distance Learning Librarianship Among Libraries with Distance Learning Librarianship Staff, Broken Out by Carnegie Class

Carnegie Class	Mean	Median	Minimum	Maximum
Community College	1.00	1.00	0.50	2.00
4-Year Degree Granting College	2.25	1.50	1.00	5.00
MA or PhD Granting College	0.98	1.00	0.25	2.50
Research University	1.26	0.95	0.10	6.00

Table 12.4: Mean, Median, Minimum and Maximum Number of FTE Positions Allotted to Distance Learning Librarianship Among Libraries with Distance Learning Librarianship Staff, Broken Out by Public or Private Status

Public or Private Status	Mean	Median	Minimum	Maximum
Public College	1.25	1.00	0.10	6.00
Private College	1.06	1.00	0.50	2.00

Table 12.5: Mean, Median, Minimum and Maximum Number of FTE Positions Allotted to Distance Learning Librarianship Among Libraries with Distance Learning Librarianship Staff, Broken Out by Number of FTE Students at the Institution

Number of FTE Students at the Institution	Mean	Median	Minimum	Maximum
>12,000	1.47	1.00	0.25	5.00
6,001-12,000	1.45	1.00	0.10	6.00
2,500-6,000	0.86	1.00	0.20	2.00
<2500	0.94	1.00	0.50	2.00

Table 12.6: Annual Salary of the Librarian Dedicated Largely to Distance Learners or who Heads a Distance Learning Librarianship Team or Division Among Libraries with Such a Position, in US$

	Less than $40,000	$40,000+ to $50,000	$50,000+ to $65,000	$65,000+ to $85,000	More than $85,000
Entire Sample	14.89%	34.04%	27.66%	19.15%	4.26%

138

Table 12.7:   Annual Salary of the Librarian Dedicated Largely to Distance Learners or who Heads a Distance Learning Librarianship Team or Division Among Libraries with Such a Position, in US$, Broken Out by U.S. and Non-U.S. Libraries

U.S. and Non-U.S. Libraries	Less than $40,000	$40,000+ to $50,000	$50,000+ to $65,000	$65,000+ to $85,000	More than $85,000
U.S.	14.29%	42.86%	20.00%	17.14%	5.71%
Non-U.S.	16.67%	8.33%	50.00%	25.00%	0.00%

Table 12.8:   Annual Salary of the Librarian Dedicated Largely to Distance Learners or who Heads a Distance Learning Librarianship Team or Division Among Libraries with Such a Position, in US$, Broken Out by Carnegie Class

Carnegie Class	Less than $40,000	$40,000+ to $50,000	$50,000+ to $65,000	$65,000+ to $85,000	More than $85,000
Community College	0.00%	40.00%	20.00%	30.00%	10.00%
4-Year Degree Granting College	25.00%	25.00%	25.00%	25.00%	0.00%
MA or PhD Granting College	5.88%	47.06%	29.41%	11.76%	5.88%
Research University	31.25%	18.75%	31.25%	18.75%	0.00%

Table 12.9:   Annual Salary of the Librarian Dedicated Largely to Distance Learners or who Heads a Distance Learning Librarianship Team or Division Among Libraries with Such a Position, in US$, Broken Out by Public or Private Status

Public or Private Status	Less than $40,000	$40,000+ to $50,000	$50,000+ to $65,000	$65,000+ to $85,000	More than $85,000
Public College	17.14%	25.71%	31.43%	22.86%	2.86%
Private College	8.33%	58.33%	16.67%	8.33%	8.33%

Table 12.10: Annual Salary of the Librarian Dedicated Largely to Distance Learners or who Heads a Distance Learning Librarianship Team or Division Among Libraries with Such a Position, in US$, Broken Out by Number of FTE Students at the Institution

Number of FTE Students at the Institution	Less than $40,000	$40,000+ to $50,000	$50,000+ to $65,000	$65,000+ to $85,000	More than $85,000
>12,000	6.25%	50.00%	31.25%	6.25%	6.25%
6,001-12,000	20.00%	20.00%	20.00%	40.00%	0.00%
2,500-6,000	16.67%	25.00%	25.00%	25.00%	8.33%
<2,500	22.22%	33.33%	33.33%	11.11%	0.00%

Table 12.11: Annual Salary of the Librarian Dedicated Largely to Distance Learners or who Heads a Distance Learning Librarianship Team or Division Among Libraries with Such a Position, in US$, Broken Out by Number of FTE Distance Learners

Number of FTE Distance Learners	Less than $40,000	$40,000+ to $50,000	$50,000+ to $65,000	$65,000+ to $85,000	More than $85,000
>2,000	11.11%	33.33%	11.11%	44.44%	0.00%
1,000-2,000	16.67%	33.33%	25.00%	25.00%	0.00%
250-999	16.67%	50.00%	16.67%	0.00%	16.67%
<250	22.22%	33.33%	33.33%	0.00%	11.11%

Table 12.12: Annual Salary of the Librarian Dedicated Largely to Distance Learners or who Heads a Distance Learning Librarianship Team or Division Among Libraries with Such a Position, in US$, Broken Out by Percentage of Distance Learners Living More than 50 Miles from Campus

Percentage of Distance Learners Living More than 50 Miles from Campus	Less than $40,000	$40,000+ to $50,000	$50,000+ to $65,000	$65,000+ to $85,000	More than $85,000
80-100%	14.29%	42.86%	14.29%	28.57%	0.00%
51-79%	10.00%	40.00%	30.00%	20.00%	0.00%
25-50%	20.00%	30.00%	30.00%	20.00%	0.00%
1-24%	14.29%	28.57%	42.86%	0.00%	14.29%

Other Reports from Primary Research Group, Inc.

THE SURVEY OF LIBRARY DATABASE LICENSING PRACTICES
ISBN: 1-57440-093-2   Price: $80.00   Publication Date: December 2007
The study presents data from 90 libraries – corporate, legal, college, public, state, and nonprofit libraries – about their database licensing practices. More than half of the participating libraries are from the U.S., and the rest are from Canada, Australia, the U.K., and other countries. Data are broken out by type and size of library, as well as for overall level of database expenditure. The 100+-page study, with more than 400 tables and charts, presents benchmarking data enabling librarians to compare their library's practices to peers in many areas related to licensing. Metrics provided include: percentage of licenses from consortiums, spending on consortium dues, time spent seeking new consortium partners, number of consortium memberships maintained; growth rate in the percentage of licenses obtained through consortiums; expectation for consortium purchases in the future; number of licenses, growth rate in the number of licenses, spending on licenses for directories, electronic journals, ebooks, and magazine/newspaper databases; future spending plans on all of the above; price inflation experienced for electronic resources in business, medical, humanities, financial, market research, social sciences and many other information categories; price inflation for ebooks, electronic directories, journals and newspaper/magazine databases; percentage of licenses that require passwords; percentage of licenses that have simultaneous access restrictions; spending on legal services related to licenses; and much more.

THE INTERNATIONAL SURVEY OF INSTITUTIONAL DIGITAL REPOSITORIES
ISBN: 1-57440-090-8   Price: $89.50   Publication Date: November 2007
The study presents data from 56 institutional digital repositories from 11 countries, including the U.S., Canada, Australia, Germany, South Africa, India, Turkey and other countries. The 121-page study presents more than 300 tables of data and commentary and is based on data from higher education libraries and other institutions involved in institutional digital repository development. In more than 300 tables and associated commentary, the report describes norms and benchmarks for budgets, software use, manpower needs and deployment, financing, usage, marketing and other facets of the management of international digital repositories. The report helps to answer questions such as: who contributes to the repositories and on what terms? Who uses the repositories? What do they contain and how fast are they growing in terms of content and end use? What measures have repositories used to gain faculty and other researcher participation? How successful have these methods been? How has the repository been marketed and cataloged? What has been the financial impact? Data are broken out by size and type of institution for easier benchmarking.

ACADEMIC LIBRARY WEBSITE BENCHMARKS
ISBN: 1-57440-094-0   Price: $85.00   Publication Date: January 2008
This report is based on data from more than 80 academic libraries in the U.S. and Canada. The 125+-page study presents detailed data on the composition of the academic library Web staff, relations with the college and library information technology departments, use of consultants and freelancers, budgets, future plans, Website marketing methods, Website revision plans, usage statistics, use of software, development of federated search and online forms and much more. Data are broken out by enrollment size, public and private status, Carnegie Class, as well as for libraries with or without their own Web staff.

PREVAILING & BEST PRACTICES IN ELECTRONIC AND PRINT SERIALS MANAGEMENT
ISBN: 1- 57440-076-2   Price: $80.00   Publication Date: November 2005
This report looks closely at the electronic and print serials procurement and management practices of 11 libraries, including: the University of Ohio, Villanova University, the Colorado School of Mines, Carleton College, Northwestern University, Baylor University, Princeton University, the University of Pennsylvania, the University of San Francisco, Embry-Riddle Aeronautical University and the University of Nebraska Medical Center. The report looks at both electronic and print serials and includes discussions of the following issues: selection and management of serials agents, including the negotiation of payment; allocating the serials budget by department; resolving access issues with publishers; use of consortiums in journal licensing; invoice reconciliation and payment; periodicals binding, claims, check-in and management; serials department staff size and range of responsibilities; serials management software; use of open access archives and university depositories; policies on gift subscriptions, free trials and academic exchanges of publications; use of electronic serials/catalog linking technology; acquisition of usage statistics; cooperative arrangements with other local libraries and other issues in serials management.

CREATING THE DIGITAL ART LIBRARY
Price: $80.00   Publication Date: October 2005
This special report looks at the efforts of 10 leading art libraries and image collections to digitize their holdings. The study reports on the efforts of the National Gallery of Canada, Cornell University's Knight Resource Center, the University of North Carolina, Chapel Hill; the Smithsonian Institution Libraries, the Illinois Institute of Technology, the National Archives and Records Administration, McGill University, Ohio State University, the Cleveland Museum of Art, and the joint effort of Harvard, Princeton, the University of California, San Diego, the University of Minnesota and others to develop a union catalog for cultural objects.

Among the issues covered: cost of outsourcing, cost of in-house conversions, the future of 35mm slides and related equipment, use of ARTstor and other commercial services, ease of interlibrary loan in images and the creation of a union catalog, prioritizing holdings for digitization, relationship of art libraries to departmental image collections, marketing image collections, range of end-users of image collections, determining levels of access to the collection, digitization and distribution of backup materials on artists lives and times, equipment selection, copyright, and other issues in the creation and maintenance of digital art libraries.

TRENDS IN MANAGEMENT OF LIBRARY SPECIAL COLLECTIONS IN FILM AND PHOTOGRAPHY

ISBN: 1-57440-001-01   Price: $80.00:   Publication Date: October 2005

This special report looks at the management and development of America's thriving special collections in film and photography. The report profiles the following collections: the University of Louisville, the Photographic Archives, the University of Utah's Multimedia Collection, The American Institute of Physics' Emilio Segre Visual Archives, the Newsfilm Library at the University of South Carolina, the University of California, Berkeley Pacific Film Archive; the UCLA Film and Television Archive, the Vanderbilt University Television News Archive, the National Archives and Records Administration's Special Media Preservation Laboratory; the University of Washington's Digital Initiatives.

The report covers digitization of photographs and film, special collection marketing, collection procurement, funding and financing, approaches for optimizing both sales revenues and educational uses, development of Web-based sale and distribution systems for photography and film, systems to assure copyright compliance, the development of online searchable databases, and many other aspects of film and photography special collections management.

THE MARKETING OF HISTORIC SITES, MUSEUMS, EXHIBITS AND ARCHIVES

ISBN: 1-57440-074-6   Price: $95.00   Publication Date: June 2005

This report looks closely at how history is presented and marketed by organizations such as history museums, libraries, historical societies, and historic sites and monuments. The report profiles the efforts of the Vermont Historical Society, Hook's Historic Drug Store and Pharmacy, the Thomas Jefferson Foundation/Monticello, the Musee Conti Wax Museum of New Orleans, the Bostonian Society, the Dittrick Medical History Center, the Band Museum, the Belmont Mansion, the Kansas State Historical Society, the Computer History Museum, the Atari Virtual Museum, the Museum of American Financial History, the Atlanta History Center and the public libraries of Denver and Evansville. The study's revealing profiles, based on extensive interviews with executive directors and marketing managers of the institutions cited, provide a deeply detailed look at how history museums, sites, societies and monuments are marketing themselves.

LICENSING AND COPYRIGHT MANAGEMENT: BEST PRACTICES OF COLLEGE, SPECIAL, AND RESEARCH LIBRARIES
ISBN: 1-57440-068-1   Price: $80   Publication Date: May 2004

This report looks closely at the licensing and copyright-management strategies of a sample of leading research, college and special libraries and consortiums and includes interviews with leading experts. The focus is on electronic-database licensing, and includes discussions of the most pressing issues: development of consortiums and group buying initiatives, terms of access, liability for infringement, archiving, training and development, free-trial periods, contract language, contract-management software and time-management issues, acquiring and using usage statistics, elimination of duplication, enhancement of bargaining power, open-access publishing policies, interruption-of-service contingency arrangements, changes in pricing over the life of the contract, interlibrary loan of electronic files, copyright clearance, negotiating tactics, uses of consortiums, and many other issues. The report profiles the emergence of consortiums and group-buying arrangements.

CREATING THE DIGITAL ACADEMIC LIBRARY
ISBN: 1-57440-071-1   Price: $69.50   Publication Date: July 2004

This report looks closely at the efforts of more than 10 major academic libraries to develop their digital assets and deal with problems in the area of librarian time management, database selection, vendor relations, contract negotiation and tracking, electronic-resources funding and marketing, technical development, archival access, open access publishing agit prop, use of ebooks, digitization of audio and image collections and other areas of the development of the digital academic library. The report includes profiles of Columbia University School of Medicine, the Health Sciences Complex of the University of Texas, Duke University Law Library, the University of Indiana Law Library, the University of South Carolina, the University of Idaho, and many others.

COLLEGE ALUMNI RELATIONS BENCHMARKS
Price: $295.00   Publication Date: 2007

This report gives critical data about the alumni relations efforts of North American colleges. In more than 115 pages and 400 tables, the study presents hard data on alumni affairs' office budgets, marketing expenditures, use of print publications and the Internet, directory building and fundraising activities, among other topics. The report, based on data from 60 colleges, gives the end-user highly specific benchmarking data such as the percentage of alumni that participate in reunions, earning from insurance plans and credit cards offered to alumni, spending on promotional materials for alumni clubs, percentage of alumni for whom the college maintains a working email address, and hundreds of other useful benchmarks and data points. Useful benchmarks include alumni office staff size, staff time spent on specific tasks, impact of the Internet on alumni communications, relations with the Office of Institutional Advancement, plans for the print directory and much more. Data are broken out for public and private colleges and by size and type of college and by size of the overall alumni population.

THE SURVEY OF DISTANCE LEARNING PROGRAMS IN HIGHER EDUCATION, 2007-08 EDITION
ISBN: 1-57440-087-8   Price: $129.50

The study is based on data from 45 higher education distance learning programs, with mean revenues of approximately $2.35 million. Data are broken out by size and type of college, for public and private colleges and for high, medium and low growth enrollment distance learning programs. The 200-page report presents more than 750 tables of data exploring many facets of distance learning programs, including revenues, cost structure, rates of pay, student demographics, program growth rates, current and planned use of new technologies, catering to special populations, and many other financial and business aspects of managing distance learning programs.

THE SURVEY OF COLLEGE MARKETING PROGRAMS
Price: $265.00   Publication Date: 2007

This report is based on detailed interviews with 55 American colleges. The report presents hard data on use of and spending on a broad range of promotional vehicles, including direct mail, Web ads and Website sponsorships, email broadcasts, blog monitoring, search engine placement enhancement, newspaper and magazine ads, billboards, television and radio advertising, Website development and other forms of advertising.

The study also presents findings on use of and spending by colleges on marketing consultants such as market research agencies, public relations firms and advertising agencies, among others. In addition, the report explores the management and organization of the college's branding and promotional efforts, exploring the degree of centralization and other issues in the management of the college marketing effort.

TRENDS IN TRAINING COLLEGE FACULTY, STUDENTS & STAFF IN COMPUTER LITERACY
ISBN: 1-57440-085-1   Price: $67.50   Publication Date: April 2007

This report looks closely at how nine institutions of higher education are approaching the question of training faculty, staff and students in the use of educationally oriented information technologies. The report helps answer questions such as: what is the most productive way to help faculty master new information technologies? How much should be spent on such training? What are the best practices? How should distance learning instructors be trained? How formal, and how ad-hoc, should training efforts be? What should be computer literacy standards among students? How can subject-specific computer literacy be integrated into curriculums? Should colleges develop their own training methods, buy packaged solutions, find them on the Web?

Organizations profiled include: Brooklyn Law School, Florida State University College of Medicine, Indiana University Southeast, Texas Christian University, Clemson University, the Teaching & Learning Technology Group, the Appalachian College Association, Tuskegee Institute and the University of West Georgia.

THE SURVEY OF LIBRARY CAFÉS
ISBN: 1-57440-089-4   Price: $75.00   Publication Date: 2007

The Survey of Library Cafés presents data from more than 40 academic and public libraries about their cafés and other foodservice operations. The 60-page report gives extensive data and commentary on library café sales volume, best-selling products, impacts on library maintenance costs, reasons for starting a café, effects on library traffic, and many other issues regarding the decision to start and manage a library café.

CORPORATE LIBRARY BENCHMARKS, 2007 Edition
ISBN: 1-57440-084-3   Price: $189.00

This report, our sixth survey of corporate libraries, presents a broad range of data, broken out by size and type of organization. Among the issues covered are: spending trends on books, magazines, journals, databases, CD-ROMs, directories and other information vehicles, plans to augment or reduce the scope and size of the corporate library, hiring plans, salary spending and personnel use, librarian research priorities by type of subject matter, policies on information literacy and library education, library relations with management, budget trends, breakdown in spending by the library versus other corporate departments that procure information, librarian use of blogs and RSS feeds, level of discounts received from book jobbers, use of subscription agents, and other issues of concern to corporate and other business librarians.

EMERGING ISSUES IN ACADEMIC LIBRARY CATALOGING & TECHNICAL SERVICES
ISBN: 1-57440-086-X   Price: $72.50   Publication Date: April 2007

This report presents nine highly detailed case studies of leading university cataloging and technical service departments. It provides insights into how they are handling 10 major changes facing them, including: the encouragement of cataloging productivity; impact of new technologies on and enhancement of online catalogs; the transition to metadata standards; the cataloging of Websites and digital and other special collections; library catalog and metadata training; database maintenance, holdings, and physical processing; managing the relationship with acquisitions departments; staff education; and other important issues. Survey participants represent academic libraries of varying sizes and classifications, with many different viewpoints. Universities surveyed are: Brigham Young; Curry College; Haverford College; Illinois, Louisiana and Pennsylvania State Universities; University of North Dakota; University of Washington; and Yale University.

EMERGING BEST PRACTICES IN LEGAL RECORDS MANAGEMENT
Price: $295.00   Publication Date: March 2006

This special report is based on detailed interviews with records managers, practice management directors and partners in major law firms and other legal offices. Among the organizational participants are: Kaye Scholer, Fulbright & Jawarski, Kilpatrick Stockton, Thomas Cooley Law School , the National Archives & Records Administration, Thompson Hine, Dewey Ballantine and Blackwell Sanders Peper Martin.

Among the issues covered in detail: Records Department Staff Size, Budget & Range of Responsibilities, Breakdown of Employee Time Use, Space Benchmarks for Offsite storage, Classification Scheme and Planning for Records Retrieval, Integration of Records with Copyright Information, Emails, Correspondence and other Forms of Legal Information, Types of Knowledge Management Software/Systems Under Consideration, Uses of Records Request Tracking, Strategies for Employee and Attorney Training in Content Control, USE of RFID & Barcoding Technology, Pace & Cost of Records Digitization, Digitization Technology & Storage Options, Records Security & Password Strategy, Relations Among the Library, Docket, Records Department, Information Technology Department and other Units Involved in Content/Knowledge Management and much more.

CORPORATE LIBRARY BENCHMARKS, 2005 EDITION
Price: $159.50   PDF Price: $174.50   Publication Date: October 2004
Corporate Library Benchmarks presents data from a survey of 50 major corporate and other business libraries. In more than 185 tables of data and commentary, the report charts developments in materials purchasing, use of office space, trends in use of librarian staff time, Fate of the physical library, trends in number of visitors to the library, trends in budgets, use of digital resources, role in knowledge management and many other facets of corporate librarianship. Data are broken out by major industry sector and by company size. Data contributed by many of America's leading corporations.

THE SURVEY OF LAW FIRM eMARKETING PRACTICES
Price: $295.00   Number of Tables: 120+
This study is based on a survey of 40 law firms with a mean size of 211 lawyers; data is broken out by size of law firm (by number of total lawyers) and by number of practice groups. Some data are also presented on a per-partner basis, such as spending on Website development per partner. In each firm a major marketing official answered questions regarding editorial staff, Website development and marketing, use of blogs, listservs, eNewsletters and other cyberspace promotional and information vehicles.

The report presents hard data on the use of search engine placement consultants, click-through rates on eNewsletters, number of unique visitors to the firm Website, and presents data on law firm spending plans for a broad range of eMarketing vehicles. The report presents hard data on law firm use of opt-in email, banner ads, Website sponsorship, per-click payments to Google, Yahoo, MSN and Overture, and much more.

The study also discusses the impact of Web-based press release distribution services and presents data on the number of law firms that use and plan to use such services. In addition to examining the prevailing methods of eMarketing, the report looks at law firm intentions in emerging eMarketing methods such as podcasting, Webcasting and streaming video, among others. The report presents quantitative assessment data on the usefulness of specific online directory sites such as Law.com, Findlaw.com and Superpages.com.

LAW LIBRARY BENCHMARKS, 2006-07 Edition
Price: $119.50   Publication Date: April 2006
Data are broken out for law firm, university law school, and public sector law libraries. Some data are also broken out for corporate law departments. The report provides data from more than 80 major law libraries and covers subjects such as staff size and growth, salaries and budget, spending trends in the library content budget, use of blogs, listservs and RSS feeds, spending on databases and commercial online services, use of and plans for CD-ROM, parent organization management's view of the future of the law library, assessment of attorney search skills, trends in information literacy training, use of reference tracking software, and much more.